MW00711671

#BOUNDLESS
Realizing the God in You

Other Books by Cassie F. Palmer

Coming Soon:

Seeing God in Me

Seeing God in Me Activity and Coloring Book

#BOUNDLESS
Realizing the God in You

Cassie F. Palmer

MOUNTAIN ARBOR PRESS

Mountain Arbor
PRESS
Alpharetta, GA

Although the author has made every effort to ensure that the information in this book was correct at the time of first publication, the author does not assume and hereby disclaims any liability to any party for any loss, damage, or disruption caused by errors or omissions, whether such errors or omissions result from negligence, accident, or any other cause.

Copyright © 2019 by Cassie F. Palmer

All rights reserved. No part of this book may be reproduced or transmitted in any form or by any means, electronic or mechanical, including photocopying, recording, or any information storage and retrieval system, without permission in writing from the author.

ISBN: 978-1-63183-381-6 - Paperback
eISBN: 978-1-63183-382-3 - ePub
eISBN: 978-1-63183-383-0 - mobi

Library of Congress Control Number: 2019904827

10 9 8 7 6 5 4 3 2   050719

Printed in the United States of America

♾ This paper meets the requirements of ANSI/NISO Z39.48-1992 (Permanence of Paper)

Scripture quotations marked "KJV" are taken from the Holy Bible, King James Version (Public Domain).

Scripture quotations marked "NIV" are taken from the Holy Bible, New International Version®, NIV®. Copyright © 1973, 1978, 1984 by Biblica, Inc.™ Used by permission of Zondervan. All rights reserved worldwide.

Scripture quotations marked "TLB" are from The Living Bible copyright © 1971 by Tyndale House Foundation. Used by permission of Tyndale House Publishers Inc., Carol Stream, Illinois 60188. All rights reserved. The Living Bible, TLB, and The Living Bible logo are registered trademarks of Tyndale House Publishers.

Scripture quotations marked "RSV" are from the Revised Standard Version of the Bible, copyright © 1946, 1952, and 1971 the Division of Christian Education of the National Council of the Churches of Christ in the United States of America. Used by permission. All rights reserved.

Illustrations by Brian Dennis

.

Be still and know that I am God.
—Psalm 46:10 (KJV)

To my grandchildren, Eden, JacRemon (JR), and Amyah. Throughout your lives, I urge you to follow God's lead. Always acknowledge Him and He will direct your path. I pray this book will help you understand who and whose you are, and also help you to recognize the importance of your connection to God.

To my parents, my devoted mother, Doris Dixon Fitzpatrick, and to the loving memory of my amazing father, Robert Louis Fitzpatrick Sr.

To the loving memory of my friend, Dorothy Ross.

I thank God for the many positive imprints each of you made on my life, for sharing so much love, wisdom, and for your constant encouragement.

I can do all things through Christ which strengtheneth me.
—Philippians 4:13 (KJV)

Contents

Epilogue

Instructor's Guide

Foreword

As you read #*BOUNDLESS: Realizing the God in You*, you will be reinvigorated and refreshed to do what God has called you to do in the deep and quiet places in your soul. You will bond with this author's desire to impact and make a difference in a world silenced by pain, yet daring to hope!

This book is the clarion call that you must not give up on God or your dreams. No matter the delay, you just trust that innate longing to forge ahead. Be the guardian of those precious gifts and callings in your life; do as the author has done and share your gifts to help inspire others. Share the gift God has given you, and do it with love and vigor. Just get it done and you will find peace in your soul and joy in your life.

Enjoy!

Christine James-Brown
The Gentle Gatherer of Gentle Gatherings Ministry

Preface

I give honor, praise, and thanks to God for birthing my spirit's desire to write #*BOUNDLESS: Realizing the God in You*. Writing this book was no coincidence. I believe it was all part of God's plan. As a teen, I was forever listening to my friends' and family members' problems, and providing encouragement that came straight from my heart. Somehow, it always seemed to be just the message they needed to hear. One of my high school classmates wrote a poem about me, where he said, "If you have a problem, sweet Cassie will fix it." This genuine concern for others' feelings and well-being, coupled with my desire to provide encouragement, has followed me throughout my life.

The experience I gained from positions held in church and in the workplace (including but not limited to director of Christian Education Ministry, youth advisor, Sunday school teacher, statewide director, and coordinator of postsecondary student organizations) afforded me opportunities to broaden my knowledge and to sharpen my skills. I loved working with and learning from young people. I admired their eagerness to learn and to absorb new ideas. I loved seeing them blossom as they realized their talents and understood their capabilities. I especially loved it when they realized they could achieve anything they believed they could because their limitations were all self-imposed. I was always applauded for encouraging and motivating the young people I was privileged to work with. These experiences, which were later coupled with questions and observations from my own children and grandchildren, propelled me to write this book to help young people understand and appreciate their inner strength.

Acknowledgments

The inspiration to undertake *#BOUNDLESS: Realizing the God in You* came from divine guidance. I was always told that when God gives you something to do, He will put the right people in your path to help you accomplish the goal. With this in mind, I thank the following people for believing in me: my husband, Sanford; my son, Sanford Jr.; Teria Coverson, whom I love as a daughter. Very special thanks to my daughter, Telicia, for her never-ending support, encouragement, suggestions, and constant reviews of my rewrites. Thanks also to my illustrator, Brian Dennis.

Love you all!

Introduction

#BOUNDLESS: *Realizing the God in You* is the result of my life-
long burning aspiration to continue inspiring young people
ourselves. I want you to understand you are God's chil-
there is a divine purpose for your lives. Though you will
with many trials, you should not give up. There are no
what you can achieve in life, because God has equipped
everything you need to handle adversity and realize all
eams. I encourage you to read and obey God's Word and
at all the answers to life's concerns, as well as the keys to
ss and success, are within you. It is important you realize
eve 1 Corinthians 3:16: "Know ye not that ye are the temple
of God, and that the Spirit of God dwelleth in you?" (KJV).

Using biblical examples and personal experiences, this book
will help you to realize how wonderful and capable you are. You
will understand that you are God's children, and that when you
acknowledge Him and put Him first in your lives, there is no limit
to what you can accomplish. You should no longer doubt your
strengths and instead affirm that the answer to any challenges you
will confront in life can be found in God's Word. You should realize
that your gifts are to be used to glorify God.

In addition, this book includes three poems I have written to
correspond to the messages in their respective chapters. The first
poem, entitled "From Within," introduces the book by pointing out
that you are connected to God through spirit and He has given you
all you need to succeed. You just need to be still and know He is the
source of all your good.

Chapter 1: Understanding Who You Are is followed by the poem entitled "See Me; Love Me." This poem points out that your physical beauty is not the most important part of you. You all are beautiful because you are made in God's image. The main thing that matters is love, and when God's love flows through you to others, they will see God's love in you.

"And You Think You Got SWAGGA" is included at the end of Chapter 5: Spiritual Warfare. The purpose of this poem is to illustrate that "glitz and glamour" are not important. It stresses Jesus's good deeds toward mankind to encourage you to love others as Jesus loves you.

At the end of each chapter, I have included additional related scriptures. These should generate even more discussions about the subject matter and allow you to dig deeper into the Bible to obtain a better understanding of the information presented in each chapter. Many of the scriptures are from the Living Bible Version (TLB) because it is simple and easy to understand. However, I have also included scriptures from the King James (KJV), New International (NIV), and Revised Standard Versions (RSV). Many of the translations were taken from The Guideposts Parallel Bible.

Food for Thought/Reflections sections are also included at the end of each chapter. These highlight the main points in each chapter and provide an opportunity for you to apply the information to situations in your life.

From Within

God grants you inner peace and access to His Power
He says it is all for you; you can call Him any hour.
Deep within your spirit, He calmly speaks to you;
If you just listen, He will guide you through.
From within, He has given you all you need to succeed.
He only asks that you listen and be open to receive.
Don't ever doubt your talents or your abilities.
God blessed you with all these things,
So take hold of your angels' wings;
Listen to your inner voice, and He will tell you how and when
As He speaks to you gently, from within.

Understanding Who You Are

Chapter 1

You are the light
of the world.

— Matthew 5:14 (NIV)

You were born into the technology age! You tweet, you text, you blog about everything and everybody. You even keep in touch with your friends through Facebook and Instagram. Without much effort, you can connect to anybody, anywhere. Though you have mastered this wonderful technological age, have you connected to God's Word? Are you in touch with who you are? Do you exhibit good character? Are you proud of who you are? More importantly, are you the person God wants you to be? Many of you probably wonder about these type questions but have no clue how to find the answers.

Some of you might think the answer to discovering who you are is found in the sports arena. You may compare yourselves to popular athletes and think you should be exactly like them. Just because you can hoop, you think you are LeBron James. If you are good with a football, you think you are Kevin Johnson, or if tennis is your game, you think you are Serena Williams. Although these individuals are all athletes and might share some common qualities, in their own ways, they are different from one another. You cannot define who you are by comparing yourself to others. Just as each of these athletes is different, you too have special qualities and talents that are uniquely yours.

Others of you look to hip-hop and television to find the answer. You listen to popular rappers and singers, but many of them devalue you and diminish your self-worth by calling you derogatory names. You also watch TV shows that offer you unrealistic portrayals of life by glorifying dangerous lifestyles and unhealthy choices. These damaging messages often confuse you with a false sense of reality. You should not define who you are by comparing yourself to these negative perceptions of what someone else tells you.

To find out who you really are, you need to look in the right places. You would not go to the club looking for your soul mate, and you would not go to church expecting the choir to sing the number-one hip-hop song, would you? If you truly want to know who you are, the best place to look is in God's Word.

For some of you, the answer to understanding who you are just might be within your hobbies and interests. These could very well be the areas in which your gifts lie. However, there are more positive sources you can use to find the inspiration you need to propel yourself forward.

One way to get encouragement through music and identify with positive messages is to listen to inspirational music. There are several radio stations that play uplifting songs that almost always address some concerns or issues you might be facing. Inspirational songs are also a good way to brighten up your day. When you hear the lyrics and the tempo of the music, you feel happy and content. Gospel is one genre where you can find songs that will uplift your spirit. Many of these songs address issues you face every day. You are a master at finding music on the internet, so google inspirational and/or gospel songs, or look them up on YouTube, then listen to them on your cell phone or other electronic devices. Try it—I think you will like it!

In your quest to understand who you are, take note that the scriptures say you are a child of God and that God has given you everything you need to sustain yourself. When He created you, He knew exactly what He was doing. To ensure your wholeness, He made you in His image. Therefore, everything about you is beautiful! Your beauty encompasses your physical beauty, how you look on the outside, and your inward beauty, things that are in your heart. Your inward beauty can be seen in how you treat others, including the love you show through kind deeds. Now that's deep! You are probably wondering, how can He do all of this? It is simple: He is an Awesome God! He is all, has all, and knows all. Yes, He is all that!

God's love for beauty can be seen all around you. His wonders can also be seen throughout nature. Look at the trees, the oceans, and the birds. At first glance, all trees might look the same, but a closer look will show that each one has its own distinct quality. Oak trees and pine trees are both woody perennials. Both vary in sizes, ranging from shrubs to heights of more than one hundred feet for oak trees and about two hundred feet for pine trees. Oak trees grow slower than pine trees and can live two hundred to four hundred years. The leaves on oak trees are usually green, but the scarlet oak has leaves that turn a brilliant red in autumn. The leaves on pine trees are also green, but they are needles that grow in bundles of two, three, or five each (*World Book Encyclopedia*, vol. 14 and 15 [1985], 474–476; 420–423). In spite of these differences, they are all still trees.

To further see God's splendor, take a look at the oceans. The Atlantic and the Pacific are both oceans. They each make the same soothing sound, yet they are different. The Atlantic is the second largest of five oceans in the world. It is also the most important ocean for commerce because the world's largest industrial countries lie along its coast. This ocean covers about one-third of the world's water surface and about one-fifth of the surface of the earth. It touches Europe and Africa on its eastern side. It covers about 31.53 million square miles and provides about one-third of the world's yearly catch of fish and shellfish (*World Book Encyclopedia*, vol. 1, 828–829).

The Pacific is the largest and deepest body of water. It is about 63.8 million square miles and covers more than one-third of the surface of the world. The floor of the Pacific is a storehouse for minerals. Though the waters of the Pacific can be calm, some of the most destructive storms on earth, including typhoons and tsunamis, start in the Pacific Ocean. Its waters reach the coast of all continents except Africa and Europe (*World Book Encyclopedia*, vol. 15, 13–15).

Both of these oceans provide some of the same natural resources, which include oil, gas fields, sand, and gravel aggregates. While they both contain fish, whaling fleets operate in the far northern and far southern parts of the Pacific Ocean. Other products contained in the Pacific Ocean include pearls, sealskins, and tropical fish for aquariums (*World Book Encyclopedia*, vol. 15, 15). Note that while they have both similarities and differences, neither is more valuable than the other.

There are approximately 8,600 types of birds. While they are all birds, they each have qualities unique to their species. All of them have feathers and wings, but they vary in size. The bee hummingbird is the smallest bird, and the ostrich is the largest. Birds also vary in color: cardinals are red; painted buntings are multicolored. While most birds fly, some of them (penguins and ostriches) do not. Some sing (canaries) and some talk (parakeets) (*World Book Encyclopedia*, vol. 2, 250–251).

Are you beginning to see the picture? From these examples, you should be able to see that you are God's greatest creation. He made you to be the person you are. You might look differently from your brother, your sister, and your best friend. You might be taller or shorter, slimmer or heavier, lighter or darker, but it is okay. You might act differently, but it is still okay. If He miraculously created nature with its entire splendor, can't you see how He created your inward and outward beauty, a beauty that is uniquely yours? No one else in this whole world is exactly like you. Is it not a good feeling to know that though you are like so many people in various ways, you are also distinctively different? You have your own special talents, your own skills, that nobody can do quite like you can. Wow, this is awesome! The poem that follows this chapter illustrates that your most important attribute is not your physical appearance, but God's loving spirit inside of you.

Like the trees, oceans, and birds God created with such marvel and distinction, He so created each of you to be alike, yet different. Why? Because He knows differences are good and that it takes all of you together to make this world a good place and do all that needs to be done. You see, in His eyes, you are all His children. He does not love any one of you more than the other. He created each of you in His image and His likeness. Psalm 139:13–14 reminds you that God created everything about you and knitted you together in your mother's womb. It says to praise Him because you are "fearfully and wonderfully made" (NIV). Do you understand what this means? It means you are everything God is, and since God is everything that is good, you are also everything that is good. Since He is wholeness and happiness, love, peace, and joy, you are all these things too.

Genesis 1:24–31 tells you that after God commanded the land to produce living creatures according to their kinds, including livestock, creatures that move along the ground, and wild animals. God saw what He had done was good, so He decided to make man in His image and His likeness. "So God created man in his own image, in the image of God he created him; male and female he created them. He made man to rule over the fish in the sea, the birds in the air. He made male and female and blessed them and said to them, 'Be fruitful and increase in number; fill the earth and subdue it. Rule over the fish of the sea and the birds of the air and over every living creature that moves on the ground.' After that, God saw all that he had made, and it was very good" (NIV). Does this not illustrate how pleased God is with you?

You are beautiful in God's eyes because you are made in His image. He has given you dominion over all His other creations. This means you have supreme authority and are more important than any creature God has placed on earth. Not only do you have dominion over the fish in the sea and the birds that fly triumphantly in the sky, but He has given you dominion over all living things, both large and small, on the earth. He has put you in charge of the earth and expects you to carry out His purpose on earth, in both the physical and spiritual realm. This means spreading God's light and His truth throughout the earth. In essence, He told humanity to "Rule over My world" (Dr. Myles Munroe, *Understanding the*

Purpose and Power of Prayer [2002], 32). Why would He give you this much authority if He did not think you were special? You should never doubt or be ashamed of who you are. God created you, and as His children, you are fully equipped and capable of doing great things. You have a "lifetime warranty," and through prayer, you can contact your manufacturer (God) anytime, anyplace, and anywhere. He is your power line! You have the right to call Him up and tell Him what is on your heart.

Just as He gave Solomon a wise and discerning mind, He has also given you the ability to make choices, so be smart and choose to follow Him. I know you spend several hours per day in school, doing homework, and participating in extracurricular activities. With all your daily activities, you probably think you do not have time for anything else. But think about it—you can show the Christ in you by doing good deeds for others on a daily basis. These can be small, simple things such as babysitting your younger siblings, helping with household chores, helping a classmate understand a subject you excel in, or calling a relative or friend to see how they are doing. It can be something as simple as a smile just to acknowledge someone's presence. Or try taking a few minutes during the day to be still and think about your blessings and how good God is to you. Then take your feeling of gratitude for the love you feel and spread it around to others you encounter.

This feeling of wholesomeness, appreciation, and love will be the foundation that will ignite your inner light so it will shine brightly and others can see Christ in you. Just knowing you have helped someone should uplift your spirits and propel you to continue to reach out to others. So you see, you can take a few minutes from the twenty-four hours you have each day to demonstrate your Christlike spirit to others. Just as God showed His love for us by giving us His son, Jesus, who showed His love for us on Calvary, you too can spread this agape love to mankind by being considerate of others, showing compassion, doing good deeds, or simply speaking kind words.

Related Scriptures

Genesis 1:26–27 (TLB): "Then God said, 'Let us make a man—someone like ourselves, to be the master of all life upon the earth and in the skies and in the seas.' So God made man like his Maker, like God did God make man; man and maid did he make them."

Romans 14:7–8 (TLB): "We are not our own bosses to live or die as we might choose. Living or dying we follow the Lord. Either way we are his."

Food for Thought/Reflections

Food for Thought:

1. You are a child of the living God.
2. You are fearfully and wonderfully made.
3. You are special in God's sight.
4. There is no one exactly like you.

Reflections:

Answer each question below using examples or situations you have experienced. In your answers, talk about how you can apply the message you learned in this chapter to the examples/situations you discuss.

1. What does it mean to you to know you are a child of the living God? Discuss specific examples.
2. In what ways do you think you are like someone close to you? This could be a relative or a friend. In what ways are you different from this person? What do the differences and the similarities mean to you?
3. What does it mean to you that you are "fearfully and wonderfully made"?
4. In what ways can you personally demonstrate your Christ-like spirit to others?

See Me; Love Me

My eyes might be brown or as blue as the morning sky.
My face may be slender or full and my cheekbones might be high.
My skin tone could be white, olive, or even tan,
But God made me as He did every man.
My skin perhaps is dark as the darkest midnight, but has a perfect glow and hue.
He made me in His image, so like Him, I am beautiful too.

See Me; Love Me

My hair could be black, brown, blonde, or maybe fiery red.
It could be curly, wavy, straight, or even adorned with kinky twists on my head.
My frame could be huge or maybe it is small,
It really does not matter as long as I let the God in me stand tall.
My features might be bold or maybe they are keen.
It is still okay because as God's child, I am royalty—like a King or a Queen.

See Me; Love Me

I strive to live the way God's Word says I should do.
I try to be a beacon so His love can shine brightly through.
I want to love my brothers and sisters the way Jesus loves me and you.

See Me; Love Me

So, when I let God's love shine radiantly through,
And when the spirit in me meets the spirit in you,
When God's love on the inside of me you see,
You cannot help but to

See Me and Love Me!

FAITH FAITH FAITH FAITH FAITH FAITH

FAITH FAITH FAITH FAITH FAITH FAITH

FAITH FAITH FAITH FAITH FAITH FAITH

FAITH FAITH FAITH FAITH FAITH FAITH

Understanding God's Purpose for Your Life

Chapter 2

Many are the plans in a man's heart, but it is the Lord's purpose that prevails.

—Proverbs 19:21 (NIV)

God has given each of you special gifts that are yours and yours alone. You probably have never sat down and thought about your gifts. You might think there is nothing special or unique about you, or you might even think you do not have any gifts. Oh, how wrong you are! There are things you can do like no one else can. To some of you, your gifts are so natural you do not recognize them as gifts. You just assume everyone can do them. This might be true, but if these are your God-given gifts, though others might be able to do them, they may not be able to do them as effortlessly and precisely as you can. You may spend a lot of time trying to determine your purpose in life, only to realize it has been right there all along.

According to Romans 12:6, "God has given each of us the ability to do certain things well," meaning that each of you has specific gifts that conform to the grace God has given you. Each of you has been given gifts according to your capability, gifts that are on your level and that you can achieve. Verses 7 and 8 of this scripture specifically say, "If your gift is that of serving others, serve them well. If you are a teacher, do a good job of teaching. If you are a preacher, see to it that your sermons are strong and helpful. If God has given you money, be generous in helping others with it. If God has given you administrative ability and put you in charge of the work of others, take the responsibility seriously. Those who offer comfort to the sorrowing should do so with Christian cheer" (TLB).

Chapter 35 of the book of Exodus discusses the many gifts God gave to the people of Israel and how they used their special gifts to glorify Him. In this chapter, He instructed Moses to build the Tabernacle. This was a huge task that Moses could not complete by himself. He needed the gifts God had given to others. According to this scripture, some of the people were skilled in sewing and made fine linens and drapes for the entrance and garments for the priests. Some were skilled craftsmen and made pillars and bases; others created masterpieces from gold, silver, and bronze. Still others had the gift of leadership, so they organized the workers. Are you getting the picture? Do you see that each of these gifts was important and that everyone's gifts were needed to build the Tabernacle?

Just as in the building of the Tabernacle, it is still true today that all of you have gifts that are important and that are needed to do God's work. Some of you have the gift of song and have powerful voices and can sing in any range. Others are gifted in sports and can run a football with the speed of a gazelle. Still others have been gifted with bright minds and can solve mathematical equations with ease. Many of you are creative in other ways and can use your minds to write books and poems; others can use your hands to make quilts or create sculptures and portraits. Some of you can also develop electronic games and apps. Still others have the ability to teach, organize, landscape, or design and build highways and buildings, including skyscrapers. Though the gifts you possess are endless, they all are important and useful in this world. Are you beginning to understand that each of you has been given special things to accomplish during your lifetime?

Not only did God give you special gift(s), He expects you to use what He has given you. To illustrate how important it is to use wisely whatever gifts you have been given, let's look at Matthew 25:14–28 (TLB). This scripture tells the story of a man getting ready to take a long trip, so he called his servants together and loaned each of them money to keep for him until he returned. The amount of money he gave was based upon their abilities. To one servant, he gave $5,000, to another he gave $2,000, and to the last servant, he gave $1,000; then he left for his trip. The servant who received $5,000 immediately started to buy and sell things so he could make more money. As a result, he made another $5,000. Like the first servant, the servant who received $2,000 also worked hard and earned an additional $2,000. The third servant, unlike the other two, dug a hole and buried his $1,000 for safekeeping.

After a long trip, the man returned and summoned each servant to give an account of the money he had received. The first servant told the man he had worked hard and earned an additional $5,000 with his money, so instead of returning only $5,000, he returned $10,000. This made the man very happy. He praised the servant for his hard work and told him since he had been faithful in how he handled his money, he would be rewarded with more responsibilities. Next came the servant who received the $2,000. He told the man he had doubled the $2,000. Again, the man was pleased and praised the servant for his good work.

Then the servant who was given $1,000 came in and told the man that because he was afraid the man would not have given him his share of what he would have earned, he had buried the money. So, he returned the $1,000 he had been given. This angered the man, and he told the servant he was wicked and lazy. He said the servant could at least have put the money in the bank so it could have earned some interest. The man then took the $1,000 and gave it the servant who had $10,000.

What should this story mean to you? It should show that you are expected to be a good steward over whatever God gives you. When you use your gifts wisely, you will be rewarded. Your reward will not always be a tangible reward. In lieu of a monetary increase, you could be blessed in so many other ways, including but not limited to having a happy and harmonious family life, genuine and fulfilling relationships, numerous educational and career opportunities; success, health, and happiness, or children and grandchildren. The list is endless.

It really does not matter how large or how small you think your gifts are. You see, they are all important because all gifts God gives you are a blessing to mankind. Remember, too, that your gifts are relative. Something you may see as a burden can be turned to your advantage. For example, large gifts can sometimes be seen as obstacles when you see them in totality. If you perceive your gifts as too large, do not let the size overwhelm you and make you think they are unattainable. Though you need to understand what God has given you to do, it is important to develop a process (a road map) that will allow you to attain your goals in different phases or in small increments.

I am reminded of something I heard a long time ago that I always told my children. In essence, it said do not view huge tasks as mountains, just step back and develop a workable plan by taking each task piece by piece. By breaking the task up into smaller pieces, you are better able to focus on each part, which allows you to organize the task and see that it is attainable. When you chip off your task one piece at a time, before long, you will be able to look behind you and see that what you perceived as a huge mountain was really only a hill.

On the other hand, small gifts are just as important. Do not make the mistake of thinking that because you perceive your gifts as too small, they are not important. One way to see the value of the gifts God has given you is to find those parts of your gifts that "ignite your passion." Then you can find ways to expand those gifts by sharing them with more people and with so much love, joy, and pride that everyone will take note. Use your gifts to show your love for mankind, as God showed us His love by giving us His Son.

Regardless of how you perceive your gifts, from time to time, some of you might experience a little apprehension. Sometimes when you venture into something new or different, you automatically go into fear mode. You are uncertain about many things. You might question your ideas or even think you do not have everything you need. Every now and then, some of you might even question your ability and think you do not know enough or that you are just not ready to share your gifts with others. Sometimes, if you are not careful, you just might allow your fear to keep you from even trying.

When you really think about it, could it be your fear is based on the possibility that you just might succeed? I caution you to let go of your self-doubt and fears, because one thing is certain: if you don't try, you surely will not succeed! Be assured that no matter the size nor the nature, your gifts are important because God has given them to you to accomplish. If you start with what you have, He will provide everything else you need. Do not allow your fears or doubts to keep you from moving forward. As His children, He expects you to achieve and excel, and He has given you everything you need to do so. You may sometimes think your gifts are not really needed or that they will not be important to others, but rest assured they were given to you to be a blessing. Using your gifts is a way to honor God by sharing with others the blessings He has bestowed upon you.

This reminds me of a story I read in one of my favorite inspirational books, *With God All Things Are Possible* (Life-Study Fellowship, 1944–1967). The story is about an old man who was an engineer on an old ferry boat. The boat was dilapidated and weather beaten, but the engine room was spotless. When a stranger asked the old man why he kept the engine room so clean, he replied, "It's easy, Cap'n. It's like this. I got a glory!" This simply means that in his heart he was happy, because as unimportant as it seemed to everyone else, making sure the engine room was the cleanest and best engine room on the river was his God-given work in life. In other words, it was his glory (48). He was doing the work God had given him, and he was doing it with joy, happiness, and pride. This story is another example of how important it is to be a good steward over whatever God gives you. It further illustrates how gifts that some people might perceive as small are very important to others.

Whatever gifts God has given you, use them to glorify Him. Unlike the servant who buried his money for safekeeping, take pride in sharing your gifts freely and joyfully with others. Remember that regardless of what your purpose in life is, it is all part of God's major purpose—to love one another. Always remember that everything you do should glorify your Heavenly Father. If you do this, your reward will be great. According to the scriptures, in Exodus 9:16, God said to Moses, "But I have raised you up for this very purpose, that I might show you my power and that my name might be proclaimed in all the earth" (NIV).

Related Scriptures

1 Corinthians 12:4–6 (TLB): "Now God gives us many kinds of special abilities, but it is the same Holy Spirit who is the source of them all. There are different kinds of service to God, but it is the same Lord we are serving. There are many ways in which God works in our lives, but it is the same God who does the work in and through all of us who are his."

1 Timothy 4:14–16 (TLB): "Be sure to use the abilities God has given you through his prophets when the elders of the church laid their hands upon your head. Put these abilities to work; throw yourself into your tasks so that everyone may notice your improvement and progress. Keep a close watch on all you do and think. Stay true to what is right and God will bless you and use you to help others."

Food for Thought/Reflections

Food for Thought:

1. God has given each of you a special gift.
2. Each one of God's gifts is important, regardless of the size.
3. Your gift should be used as a blessing to others.
4. Do not allow your fear to keep you from sharing your gift.

Reflections:

Answer each question below using examples or situations you have experienced. In your answers, talk about how you can apply the message you learned in this chapter to the examples/situations you discuss.

1. What unique gift(s) has God given you?
2. Explain how you can use your gift(s) to be a blessing to others.
3. Why do you think your gift(s) from God is important?
4. Are you using your gift(s)? If not, what is keeping you from sharing what God has given you? What is your timeline to start sharing your gift?

FAITH FAITH FAITH FAITH FAITH FAITH

FAITH FAITH FAITH FAITH FAITH FAITH

The Importance of Prayer

Chapter 3

Therefore I tell you, whatever you ask for in prayer, believe that you have received it, and it will be yours.

—Mark 11:24 (NIV)

Prayer is your gateway to Heaven. It is the channel through which you can communicate with God. To use an analogy, let's think of prayer as a pipeline. A pipeline can be used to efficiently carry water, oil, natural gas, and various fluids over a long distance, but it can also refer to a source from which you can obtain information. Prayer, like a pipeline, is the channel that allows for the flow of information between you and God. It also allows you an opportunity to petition God for your requests. At the same time, prayer is a source that allows you to both talk to and hear from God. When you pray, you can go to God in secret and know your prayers are heard.

Prayer is your private time with God where you can truthfully discuss your problems, admit your shortcomings, and ask for His divine guidance. Before you ask, God already knows what you need. Your prayers do not need to be long; they need only to be simple, specific, and sincere. When you pray, you are simply having a conversation with God. You know the respect and love you show when you talk to your earthly father? Well, you can talk to your Heavenly Father in the same way. You do not need to have perfect diction to talk to God. You do not need to be Daniel Webster or a master of the English language. You just need to honestly talk to God and approach Him with a pure heart.

You can go to God in prayer with anything and everything. The list of reasons to pray is inexhaustible. It can include when you are feeling happy or sad, when you need strength, when you are sick, when you are tempted to do something you know is not right, or even when you are afraid. You can pray a prayer of thanksgiving, when you are praising and thanking God for all He has done, is doing, or will do in your life. You can pray to God as an intercessor for someone else, meaning you are praying to God on their behalf.

Though there is no right or wrong way to pray, the Bible instructs you in Matthew 6:6 to "go away by yourself, all alone, and shut the door behind you and pray to your Father secretly, and your Father, who knows your secrets, will reward you" (TLB). This means you should find your special "quiet" place where you can go and be relaxed and comfortable so you can talk to God. This should be a place where you can open your heart to God and let everything flow out. Your special place can be your bedroom, it can be a closet, a corner in the kitchen, or under the big oak tree in the backyard. The point I am trying to make is that it really does not matter, so long as it is a place where you can be at peace. Think about this for a while. Once you have identified your special place, go there and spend some time talking freely and secretly to God about whatever is on your heart. God already knows all your secrets, so go ahead and talk to Him.

You also need to know there is no special way, time of day, or place to pray. You can pray to God while you are sitting, standing, on your knees, or lying down. You can be in church, in your room, at school, or anywhere. You can pray in the morning, afternoon, or at night. The main thing for you to understand is that it does not matter where, when, how, or how long you pray. Your prayers do not need to be long to be powerful. Prayers are powerful when you pray using His words. This means you can quote scriptures from the Bible that relate to whatever situation you might be going through.

What is important is that you take time to talk to God through prayer and that you believe all prayers in Jesus's name will be answered according to God's will. God will listen to you and He will guide you in the way best suited for you. God likes it when you come to Him in prayer as you are reminded in Luke 11:10: "Everyone who asks, receives; all who seek, find; and the door is opened to everyone who knocks" (TLB).

According to 1 Timothy 2:1–2, you are instructed to pray for everyone, including those who have authority over you. When you pray, you should ask God to have mercy upon them and also thank Him for what He is doing for them. God tells us in verse 5 of this scripture that He "is on one side and all the people on the other side, and Christ Jesus, himself man, is between them to bring them together" (TLB). This means the only way you can get to God is through His son, Jesus. If you truly believe with all your heart that Jesus is the son of God, that He died for your sins and arose from the dead, then you will not have any problems knowing Jesus holds the key that will unlock the door that leads to His Father.

Have you ever prayed for something over and over and thought you would never get an answer? Did you think maybe you were not praying hard enough or long enough? Did you set a time frame during which you thought you should have received an answer from God, but you did not receive one? Did the wait make you think maybe God just does not answer all prayers, or perhaps He picks and chooses the ones He wants to answer? You might even think, He just does not answer prayers. Let's just take a few minutes and talk about this.

God truly does answer all prayers. He may not answer them within the time frame you would like, or in the way you might expect. When you ask God for something, be it guidance, healing, or forgiveness, He hears you. God is God all by Himself; He does not need you to tell Him when to do something, nor do you need to tell Him what to do. Since He is wise and knows all things, He will answer you in His own time. The answer you receive might not be the answer you want, but since God knows you better than you know yourself, the answer you receive will be the answer you need.

This reminds me of something that happened several years ago when I prayed for a certain job. When I was not selected, at first I was disappointed, but then I realized it was a blessing. This job, though the salary was great, was more demanding than the one I had. It would have required longer working hours, more of my time, more responsibility, and more stress. It was during this time that my husband became critically ill and needed me to stay close by his side. I had to take a leave of absence to attend to his medical needs. The stress of a new job coupled with the stress of my husband's illness would have been an enormous task for me. God, in

His infinite wisdom, knew all this was going to happen and that I was better off without the new job. You see, I did not get the answer I wanted, but I got the right answer. I got what God willed for my life at the time.

To further illustrate the power of prayer, in November 2005, our daughter, who was perfectly healthy, became suddenly ill while visiting in Oklahoma with her husband's family for Thanksgiving. On November 24, after returning home from our family's Thanksgiving dinner, my husband and I received a telephone call from our son-in-law informing us that our daughter had been taken to the emergency room because she was not feeling well. According to him, it was nothing serious; they just wanted to watch her overnight, and she would be released the next morning. A few hours later, we received a call from one of the nurses who said our daughter had developed a fever. They had given her antibiotics and she would be fine, but they wanted her to remain in the hospital for three to five days for observation. During the night, we received another call from a nurse who said her fever was elevating and they did not know why, so they were putting her in CCU for closer observation. I asked if we should come to Oklahoma and was told we could if we wanted to comfort her, but they thought she would be fine. I didn't like what I was hearing, so I booked my husband and I on the earliest flight we could find. On November 26, we left for Oklahoma.

During the flight, I opened my inspirational book, and there was a Daily Word inside. I just opened it without searching for a particular prayer. The prayer on the page was entitled "God's message of comfort reassures me that all is well." As I read the prayer, I was inspired by the last line: "My order is at work for you. My love is pouring out upon you. Rest in this assurance, my beloved: I am here, and all is well." I immediately wrote a note thanking God for the confirmation that He had heard my prayer. I turned to my husband and said, "I have received confirmation that God is already in Oklahoma and our child is healed." It was this peace that carried me to Oklahoma.

Even with all my faith, I was not prepared for what I saw at the hospital. It appeared to me that she was connected, intravenously, to everything in the room! Her stats were terrible. The doctor told us she had only a 20 percent survival rate. Her heart rate was extremely low. To keep her heart beating, a balloon pump had been placed in her chest. We were told it would only last for thirty days. The doctors informed us that she needed a heart transplant or she would not survive. She would need to be accepted in a hospital in Oklahoma City to receive the heart transplant. Several other tests were needed before her acceptance could be confirmed. Each test result was worse than the one before it. One of the doctors told me he would conduct one more test, and if the results were not within a certain range, she could not be referred. I told him to do what he knew how to do and to let God do the rest.

Everybody was praying, family, friends, and people I met at the hospital. I prayed like I had never prayed before. I thanked God for her healing even while the doctors were telling me her chance of survival was slim. I quoted the scriptures that talked about the healings Jesus performed. I felt so much peace and comfort as I continuously read them to my daughter. Even though she was on life support, I believed God would heal her. I never doubted His Word. I prayed with confidence and with expectancy. I kept thinking if God performed the miracles in the Bible, He would do the same thing now. I prayed words from the Gospel According to St. John, specifically chapter 4:46–54. This chapter talks about a nobleman's faith in God's Word, as spoken through Jesus. The nobleman went to Galilee to see Jesus because his son was ill. He asked Jesus to return to Capernaum with him to heal his sick son. When Jesus told him to go home because his son was alive, the nobleman believed what Jesus said and went home. As he approached his house, his servants told him his son was alive. When the servants told the nobleman the exact time his son's health had improved, the nobleman realized this was the same time Jesus had told him (the day before) that his son was alive.

This was a trying time for our daughter and for our family, but as a result, I learned to trust God's promises even more. This was also a learning experience that reinforced in me the power of prayer and the truth of God's Word. I also learned there is power in praying God's words. As a result of my faith in God's Word and continuous prayers from the East Coast to the West Coast, she was miraculously healed and did not need a heart transplant. I can triumphantly say God's Word is true and that when you step out of your adverse situation, place your trust in God and completely turn it over to Him. He will always work it out, according to His will.

Prayer provides you with the strength to face your trials and tribulations. It serves as a mechanism to renew, expand, and relate to what the scriptures say in one of my favorite verses in the Bible, Matthew 6:25. In summary, this scripture reminds you not to worry or be anxious, because just as God takes care of the birds and the flowers, He will surely take care of you. This scripture also reminds you not to worry about tomorrow. You should leave that to God and just take one day at a time.

You should believe and remember that God's Word and His promises are true. If He says it, then it will come to pass. In other words, you can count on it. You should always remember that when you pray, you must be persistent and pray until you get results.

Related Scriptures

Philippians 4:6 (TLB): "Don't worry about anything; instead, pray about everything; tell God your needs, and don't forget to thank Him for His answers."

Jeremiah 33:3 (NIV): "Call to me and I will answer you and tell you great and unsearchable things you do not know."

Food for Thought/Reflections

Food for Thought:

1. Prayer is your pipeline to God.
2. You can always stand on God's Word and His promises.
3. You can talk to God about anything, anytime and anywhere.
4. God always answers your prayers, in His own time and according to His will.

Reflections:

Answer each question below using examples or situations you have experienced. In your answers, talk about how you can apply the message you learned in this chapter to the examples/situations you discuss.

1. Has there been a time when you prayed for a specific outcome, but the answer you received was different from what you expected? Discuss your situation and include the outcome you prayed for. What was the outcome you received?
2. Have you ever prayed and thought God would not answer your prayer because you did not receive an answer in the time frame you wanted? Discuss how you felt as you waited.
3. While praying about a specific situation, have you ever quoted God's words from scriptures that related to the situation you were praying about? Discuss your situation and how the related scripture(s) put you at peace and gave you faith that God would answer you.
4. What is your favorite place to have quiet time and prayer with God? What makes this place special for you?

FAITH FAITH FAITH FAITH FAITH FAITH FAITH FAITH FAITH FAITH FAITH FAITH FAITH FAITH FAITH FAITH FAITH FAITH FAITH FAITH

Hearing from God

Chapter 4

Be still, and know that
I am God.

—Psalm 46:10 (KJV)

Does God really talk to you? How does He talk to you? How do you know it is really Him? I am sure many of you have wrestled with these questions. It is true, God does talk to you. As discussed in the previous chapter, prayer is the major communication channel between you and God. It allows you to talk to God and also for you to hear from Him. However, while it is the major way to speak with Him, it is not the only line of communication. You see, God speaks to you in several ways, including but not limited to His Word, and through other people. He also speaks to you during various times, such as in the midst of your storms and in the stillness.

Not only does God speak to you in different ways, but He also speaks to you all the time. You do not always hear Him because you are so busy doing other things like texting, blogging, tweeting, talking on the phone, playing video games, or just going through your normal daily routines.

The main way God speaks to you is through His Word. When you are troubled, the best source of comfort is reading scripture. The Bible is a daily guide that has all the answers you are seeking. In His Word, He tells you how to approach life. He tells you about the miracles He has performed and will perform if you just believe. He tells you He is your rock and fortress and that He will guide you. He also tells you in Psalms 23 that He is your shepherd and has everything you need; He restores you, He helps you, He walks with you, and He provides for you. He even says His goodness and kindness will always be with you. In the book of Proverbs, you will find morals and ethical principles for you to live by, including listening to the things your parents tell you, trusting in God completely, putting Him first in your life, and allowing Him to direct your path. There are several other passages listed in the Bible that will guide you through life.

One other way God speaks to you is through other people. I have heard many ministers say when God has something for you to do, He will often put an idea in your spirit and He will always confirm it through others. This means God uses others to help you achieve what He wants you to do. If He tells you to do something, He confirms it by allowing other people to either say the same thing to you or assist you in achieving the task. Think about it. Who are some of the people you trust? These should be people who have provided sound advice in the past and have good intentions and sound morals. Who are the people who have provided guidance throughout your life? Who are your positive role models? I am sure you have encountered people in your life who fit these descriptions. For some of you, these people could be your parents, grandparents, siblings, other relatives, pastor, Sunday school teacher, counselor, teacher, or your next-door neighbor. My point is there are people in your inner circle who can be that beacon of hope for you during the most troubled moments of your life. They can inspire and encourage you when you need sincere guidance. These are people who have always shown you they are concerned about your well-being and who have always stood with you, protected you, and inspired you to follow your dreams. In essence, they are your cheering squad!

Not only does God speak to you through His Word and through other people, He also speaks to you during various situations, including in the midst of your storms and in the stillness. Can you think of a time when you thought everything was going wrong, and that no one, not even your mama or your best friend, understood or even cared about what you were going through? I am sure you can remember times like these. Can you remember how lonely, scared, and disappointed you felt, and how you wished you could talk to someone who would understand? Well, you do have someone who understands. You have God! You can always tell Him your troubles and always know you are not alone. He understands just what you are going through and will speak to you when you think there is no answer or no way out. I think God answers you when you are at your lowest point in an effort to get your attention so you will realize He is always with you and there is nothing too hard for Him to accomplish. He also wants you to know that while He does hear you and will always show you options, the choice is yours. While going through your storms, listen to His voice, obey His Word, and believe things will get better.

He speaks to you in the stillness, when your mind is relaxed and you are calm. This is why some people like to still themselves in nature settings. Personally, I feel that God speaks to me when I am around water. It is almost as if I can tune out all my daily challenges and concerns. I focus on the chirping, rhythmic sounds of the birds, the gentle rustling of the wind as light breezes brush my face. The calmness of the ocean waves as they glisten against the peaceful blue skies soothe me and make me feel that God is near. Like it says in the Allstate commercial, I am "in good hands."

Meditation is another way to connect with God in stillness. It is your quiet time with Him where you can be still, relax, and focus on God and His goodness. It will allow you to escape the worries of the world. It is also a way to be still and just calm yourself so you can be in tune with your spirit. In this solitude, you are more apt to be open to hear from God and feel His presence. Remember when you were a small child and how safe, secure, and happy you felt after a parent, grandparent, sibling, other family member, or even a family friend just rocked you in their arms when you were afraid or needed some reassurance? This is the same safe and secure feeling you get when you still yourself and allow God to gently speak to you. It feels good when you take a few minutes to relax, quiet your mind, and just *be*. You can use this time to forget about your concerns and worries and let your mind focus on something pleasant to you and meditate on this for a while. While in this moment, feel the peace and oneness with God. Stay here as long as you need to, and when you are ready, slowly open your eyes and feel how good and safe you felt basking in God's presence. God instructs you to do this in Psalm 46:10: "Be still, and know that I am God" (KJV). When you are still, you can focus better. Your senses are keener, and this makes you more aware of your inner feelings. You are more open to new ideas and are better able to receive what God has to say.

Meditation is a powerful method to enhance your spiritual development, and it will also help you understand that everything you will ever need throughout your life is inside of you. What this means is that you are a spiritual being, and through spirit, you are connected to God (who is spirit). Your spirit is the essence of your being. Through this connection, God is your inner core. He is the vine and you are the branches, and therefore you must stay connected to Him to be fruitful and have a good life.

Meditation is also a calming state that will allow you to reflect on pleasant things in your life. It serves as a way to release stress by providing an opportunity for a little self- examination so you can look at your own character and actions. As you meditate, you will relax and go deep within to connect with your spirit. Just meditating a few minutes per day will make a big difference in how you feel and how you approach life and its many challenges. Relax, breathe deeply, and let your worries go as you experience God's presence. This calming and powerful technique will allow you to connect with your spirit and focus on your oneness with God. It also rejuvenates your mind and opens a pathway for deeper faith and wisdom. In addition, meditation enhances awareness and wisdom, and intensifies creativity.

You can meditate any time of the day you choose, any place you choose, and as often as you would like. I like to meditate at night, in either my sunroom or my bedroom. My favorite place is actually in bed because I usually just drift off to sleep. This is the time I feel most relaxed and worry free. I am better able to tune the world out and forget the pressures of the day. To prepare for my meditations, I spray the room and my linens with a relaxing scent like jasmine or lavender. Since I do not live on the ocean (yet), I turn on my water fountain and play soothing music in the background. Then, I dim the lights or turn them off. This is my "me" time where I unwind from my busy days and connect with my spirit. It also helps if I silently repeat a word or phrase that means something to me and makes me feel at peace. It could be something as simple as the word peace or love or happy. I also visualize my favorite place, which is the ocean. Then, I just relax, breathe, and enjoy the solitude. Being in this state allows me to really focus on God. It is during this time that I try to "let go and let God." While in this calming state, I can connect to my true self and visualize the person I think God created me to be. Meditation allows me to just be and align with my spirit to open myself up to endless possibilities.

Go ahead and try it. You decide the time of day and the place where you can meditate. All that matters is that you are calm and open to receive. Connect with your inner spirit and experience the beauty, calmness, peace, and unity when you are focused on God. Once you make this connection, you will realize that everything you need, all that you are, and all that you can be is already within you.

Now I hope you see that God really does speak to you all the time and in various ways. You just need to remember that what God has to say to you is important. When you listen to Him, you will be able to understand His purpose for your life. I encourage you to slow down, clear your mind, and open your heart so you can hear His whisper. What better voice can you hear than the voice of God?

Related Scriptures

Acts 9:4–7 (TLB): "He fell to the ground and heard a voice saying to him . . . 'Who is speaking, sir?' Paul asked. And the voice replied, 'I am Jesus. . . .' The men with Paul stood speechless with surprise, for they heard the sound of someone's voice but saw no one!"

Romans 10:17 (NIV): "Consequently, faith comes from hearing the message, and the message is heard through the word of Christ."

Food for Thought/ Reflections

Food for Thought:

1. God speaks to you all the time.
2. God is the source of all your good.
3. God speaks to you in different ways.
4. God speaks to you during your storms.

Reflections:

Answer each question below using examples or situations you have experienced. In your answers, talk about how you can apply the message you learned in this chapter to the examples/situations you discuss.

1. Has God ever spoken to you through other people? If so, talk about who the person(s) was and the message you received.
2. Have you ever experienced God's voice in the stillness? If so, describe the setting and how you felt.
3. What are some other ways God has spoken to you? How did you respond?
4. Have you ever pondered over something you wanted to do but were not sure about? And then someone, who knew nothing about what you were thinking, told you the same thing? Could this have been God confirming what He wanted you to do? If this has ever happened to you, discuss your thoughts.

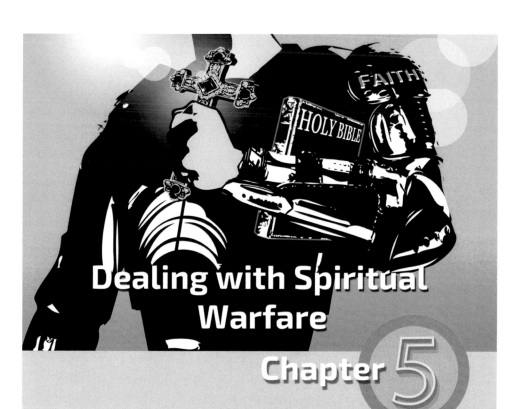

Dealing with Spiritual Warfare

Chapter 5

Be strong in the Lord and in his mighty power. Put on the full armor of God, so that you can take your stand against the devil's schemes. For our struggle is not against flesh and blood, but against the rulers, against the authorities, against the powers of this dark world and against the spiritual forces of evil in the heavenly realms.

—Ephesians 6:10–12 (NIV)

In the previous chapters, I have talked about what it means to be a child of God, how you are made in His image, and how you are capable of achieving marvelous things. I have told you that you possess unique gifts and can communicate with God through prayer about anything and at any time. I have also told you God speaks to you in various ways and that He is with you through good times and difficult times. Now, it is time to let you know that even though you are aware of all these things, you will sometimes be faced with challenges that are not physical. These will be things you cannot touch, things that are more moral than physical. As explained in chapter 6 of Ephesians, this is not a physical fight; it is fighting against evil, against things you know are wrong. These can also include things you see on a daily basis, such as a lack of concern for others' well-being, selfishness, and unfair practices and denied freedoms imposed on various groups in different societies. Regardless of the issue, this scripture tells you the strength to fight spiritual wars must come from the power of God within you. Ephesians 6 tells you how to deal with spiritual warfare. It says you must do everything you can to stand firm and that you must be appropriately dressed for this fight. What is the appropriate dress? According to this scripture, you must fight this battle with truth, righteousness, peace, faith, salvation, and the Word of God.

This chapter will provide you with the basic information concerning spiritual warfare found in the scriptures. It also includes examples of ways you might encounter spiritual warfare during your daily life and scripture references on how to handle these encounters. At the end of this chapter, I have included a poem entitled "And You Think You Got SWAGGA." This poem illustrates that life is not about you and what you think you have. It talks about Jesus's love for mankind and encourages you to live right and not to engage in violent acts. In essence, it encourages you to follow God's Word and spread love to all mankind.

Do you know you are constantly fighting a war? And that you probably are not aware of who you are fighting, or why? A spiritual war is a war where you sometimes cannot recognize the enemy. It is a war that, without the right protection, you certainly will not win! What is the right protection? It is the Word of God.

The battle you fight constantly is over good and evil; it is mankind's struggle with temptation. This is the same battle that was fought and lost by Adam and Eve in the Garden of Eden. To show you what I mean, think about all the things you are faced with every day. There are many instances in which you might need to decide between what is right and what is wrong. These are things that will test your character, your morals, and your values. Some can be as simple as the type of friends you choose, how you treat others, helping others during their times of need, and simply making sound decisions. Sometimes, your decisions are influenced by others, and they might not be the best decision for you. To illustrate this, let's use a hypothetical day in school:

Homeroom has just ended and you are on your way to your first-period class. Your friend stops you in the hall and says, "What's up? I'm not feeling school today, I'm leaving. Do you want to go?" You think about this for a few minutes. Should I stay (nothing is really happening today), or should I go (I did not do my homework last night, anyway)? Do you know what is happening here? You are fighting internally over right and wrong. You are trying to justify, or wrestling with, something you know is wrong. You know it is wrong to leave school, but because you are thinking about it, you are tempted by the idea.

First Corinthians 15:33 warns you about the company you keep. It specifically tells you that "bad company corrupts good character" (NIV). What do you do? In the final analysis, it is your decision. Your answer should be based on what you believe is right and wrong, and not what your friend thinks is right.

Just like in the Garden of Eden, both Adam and Eve disobeyed God. They knew it was wrong to eat from the tree in the center of the garden. Eve was tempted by the serpent, who told her she would not die if she ate the fruit from that tree. He told her God did not want her to eat from the tree because God knew if they ate from it, their eyes would be opened and they would know the difference between good and evil. Believing the serpent and probably thinking how good the fruit looked, Eve ate it anyway. She then carried some to Adam, and even though he too knew it was wrong to eat the fruit from the forbidden tree, he also ate it. They both gave in to temptation. As a result of Adam and Eve disobeying God, and because they gave in to the devil's temptation, they fell from God's grace. To this day, mankind still has problems resisting temptation.

You might be faced daily with decisions that will cause you to wrestle with temptation. It is still the major tool the devil uses in this spiritual battle. He will throw everything he has at you to shake your faith. He will make you think you are not smart enough to do something, when you really are; that you do not have everything you need, when you do. In other words, if you let him, the devil will rob you of your strength, your power, and your faith. To handle these types of situations, you need to know God's Word provides guidance for you. He knew you would be faced with this fight and tells you in His Word how to fight against the wickedness of the world. In Exodus 14:14, He tells you that He "will fight for you; you need only to be still" (NIV).

The Word of God also tells you how to dress to win the spiritual battle. Like any soldier in battle, you must put on the right protection. However, unlike a regular war, you will not use man-made weapons. To fight against the spiritual wickedness of the world and be standing when it is all over, you must be fully equipped with God's armor. Ephesians 6:10–18 (TLB) reminds you:

Your strength must come from the Lord's mighty power within you. Put on all of God's armor so that you will be able to stand safe against all strategies and tricks of Satan. For we are not fighting against people made of flesh and blood, but against persons without bodies — the evil rulers of the unseen world, those mighty satanic beings and great evil princes of darkness who rule this world; and against huge numbers of wicked spirits in the spirit world.

So use every piece of God's armor to resist the enemy whenever he attacks, and when it is all over, you will still be standing up.

But to do this, you will need the strong belt of truth and the breastplate of God's approval. Wear shoes that are able to speed you on as you preach the Good News of peace with God. In every battle you will need faith as your shield to stop the fiery arrows aimed at you by Satan. And you will need the helmet of salvation and the sword of the Spirit — which is the Word of God.

Pray all the time. Ask God for anything in line with the Holy Spirit's wishes. Plead with him, reminding him of your needs, and keep praying earnestly for all Christians everywhere.

To fully engage in this battle, you must be truthful and you must be righteous, meaning you must be godly and just in the things you do. You must be peaceful and also be willing to communicate to others the importance of peace. You must have faith that God will do what His Word says He will do. You must have salvation and know the Word of God. You must understand that nothing has greater power than the Word of God. If you put on the full armor of God, no matter what the devil throws at you, you will still be standing tall in the end. To win this battle, 1 John 3:8 tells you the reason the Son of God appeared was to destroy the works of the devil. To win this battle, you must be totally committed to Christ Jesus.

You also need to be aware that the closer you get to God, the more temptations you will encounter. The more you try to do right, the more others will try to persuade you to do wrong. You should also remember it is all about God and not about you, and that following His Word is not always easy, but it is always the right thing to do. Don't give up the fight, just always believe that nothing can separate you from the love of God. As the Bible tells you in Romans 8:37–39, "No, in all these things we are more than conquerors through him who loved us. For I am convinced that neither death nor life, neither angels nor demons, neither the present nor the future, nor any powers, neither height nor depth, nor anything else in all creation, will be able to separate us from the love of God that is in Christ Jesus our Lord" (NIV).

Related Scriptures

Proverbs 2:20 (TLB): "Follow the steps of the godly instead, and stay on the right paths."

Ephesians 6:11 (NIV): "Put on the full armor of God, so that you can take your stand against the devil's schemes."

Food for Thought/Reflections

Food for Thought:

1. You are at war every day of your life.
2. You are protected when you put on the full armor of God.
3. The more you try to do right, the more other people try to make you do wrong.
4. The closer you get to God, the more temptations you will encounter.

Reflections:

Answer each question below using examples or situations you have experienced. In your answers, talk about how you can apply the message you learned in this chapter to the examples/situations you discuss.

1. Can you remember a time when you thought you were under attack? Discuss, using specific details. How did you handle this situation?
2. Do you believe nothing can separate you from the love of God? Give specific examples.
3. What specific examples can you provide to show some of the things you encounter that you consider to be spiritual warfare? Explain why.
4. Why do you think putting on the full armor of God protects you?

And You Think You Got SWAGGA

'Cause you walk with a dip in your hip and a glide in your stride,
'Cause you think everyone knows you from the east to the
west side.
You think you got it going on; it's all about you.
You got a nice ride and a little change in your pocket too!
So you think you got everything and all that glitters is gold.
You want everything new; don't want nothing old.

And you think you got SWAGGA?

Well listen up and just let me 'holla' at you a minute, I want to tell
you about a man who is everything and yes, He put SWAGGA
in it!
Take a look in the Word and you will see how out of the dust of the
earth,
His Father formed Adam; took a rib from his chest and to Eve He
gave birth.
He is the beginning and the end,
He even walked on water and into Heaven He did ascend.
With two fish and five loaves of bread,
Five thousand hungry mouths He fed.
But wait a minute, He did much more than that. He healed the sick
and gave sight to the blind.
He turned water into wine and performed other miracles that will
blow your mind!
He is the wonderful counselor, the prince of peace.
His love for you will never cease.

You come to His Father only through Him.
He loves you all, whether you are heavy or slim.
He will fight your battles and show you a better way.
He will put sunshine in your heart on a cloudy day.
He is closer to you than a brother; He is your very best friend.
He will never let you down; on Him you can always depend.
He is God's only son; yes He died for your sins.
Walk in God's Word and His favor you will win.
He is the way, the truth, and the light.
Follow His teachings and you will live your life right!

And you think you got SWAGGA?

So you see it's all about Him; it's not about you.
Get your life right; you got to learn God's Word and yes, you got
    to live it too!
Stop lying, stealing, and killing your "peeps,"
Learn to show love and remember, God's commandments you
    must keep.
He expects you to honor your father and your mother.
And He wants you to love one another.
So if you want to have SWAGGA like Jesus Christ had,
Check your attitude; be happy, you really have no reason to be mad.
Develop good character and let your light so brightly shine.
Always do good deeds and show love to all mankind.
You can be unique but do it in a good way,
By striving to live right every day.

See, if you really want to get your SWAGGA on,

Don't copy the ways of violent men.
Violence leads to a life of distress and sin.
Be wise, have good judgment, and use common sense.

Don't be rebellious; exercise penitence.

Live your life as the book of Proverbs instructs.

Reverence the Lord; listen to the voice of wisdom and you will not self-destruct.

Follow God's Word and really get your SWAGGA on!

Learning through Adversity

Chapter 6

Thou therefore endure
hardness, as a good
soldier of Jesus Christ.

—2 Timothy 2:3 (KJV)

Remember a time when things were not going the way you expected, and it seemed like everything was going wrong. Maybe you tried out for the marching band and did not get selected, or you missed the school bus and had to walk to school in the rain, or your best friend stopped speaking to you. This might have made you feel like everything was just caving in all around you! Then, suddenly, you remembered someone very dear to you had always told you the sun may not be shining today, but it will surely shine again. Or sometimes this person would say to you, "Don't worry, baby, things will get better." Thinking of this brightened your day and made you feel that your situation was not as bleak as you originally thought. You realized whatever your situation might be, there is always a solution.

Life, like the weather, cannot be controlled by you. What is the weather like in your neighborhood today? Is it cloudy or is it sunny? Is it raining or is it snowing? Is it hot or is it cold? What I am trying to get you to see is that, like the weather, life is sometimes unpredictable, sometimes unsettling, and sometimes simply gorgeous. It is full of wonders, mysteries, ups, and downs. You never know what it will deal you. It is a mixture of good times, trying times, and difficult times. It can be like a box of valentine candy, filled with dark chocolates, mixed nuts, and sweet cherries. Either way, you have no control over the mixture in the box. So it is with life; you cannot control everything that happens. God never promised every day would be sunny and that there would never be rain. He never said you would always have good times and never bad times. He surely never promised you would always be happy and never be sad.

Just as the earth experiences various seasons and each season has its good days and bad days, you too will have various seasons in your life. When you are in the spring of your life, you might be at a creative point where you are experiencing new ideas and realizing your gifts. You are envisioning a bright future and recognizing that your opportunities and achievements are boundless. You will also have summers, when everything is going real good and you have no problems. Life could not be better; you are at a very high point. Your grades are good, you are involved in several extracurricular activities, and you have just been voted president of your class!

Enjoy these seasons because one day, the spring and summer will give way to the fall and winter. This simply means the sun will not shine as brightly every day. You will have some cloudy days; you may be at your lowest point and will not be sure which way to go or what to do. You will also have some cold and stormy days. There will be days when you are feeling so distraught and unsure you will feel like a ship lost at sea, and all you want to do is send out an SOS and pray that something good will happen to ease your pain. It is during these low points in your life you should realize you are not alone. You need to understand you are not the only one who will have times where you need to take a deep breath and realize that through all of your tough and perplexing times, God is right there with you! The poem "Footprints in the Sand" is a good illustration of how God understands and how He responds to you when you are going through difficult times. In this poem, the person acknowledges God's presence and recognizes that God is walking with him during his life's journey. What amazes me is when the person was at his weakest point, he thought God had deserted him. He wondered where God was when he could not make it on his own. He thought that when he could not carry his heaviest burdens, God had left him alone. My favorite part of this poem is when God tells him that when he was at his weakest point, the reason he only saw one set of footprints in the sand is because God picked him up and carried him through his storm! I get goose bumps every time I think about how awesome our God is.

Each of you will have moments or situations when you feel all alone and think no one is interested in what you are going through or how you are feeling. Since you do not know what will happen from one moment to the next, does it not make sense to be close to the only one who does know? If you read God's Word, you will find that you are not the only one who will experience hardships; each of you will have your own individual troubles. God expects you to go *through* your troubles. This means you will you get over whatever is currently happening in your life and you will realize there is a bright side to every seemingly dark situation. Knowing and believing that God is always with you gives you the hope and strength you need to keep pushing forward. When you keep trying and have faith that God will provide, you will begin to see there is a bright side to your situation. You should then begin to realize your current situation is not as bad as you perceived, and that when you do all you know how to do to fix it, you need to stop worrying and turn it over to God. Once you turn it over, then know He will see you through it and that you will rise above your current situation. The key is, you must learn to lean on God and trust that He will guide you through your trials and tribulations. Just like in the poem mentioned above, He walks with you through all your struggles and hard times. He never allows you to go through difficult situations alone.

God has a way of redirecting your path and pointing you in the right direction. Many years ago, my husband was having problems with his knees. We scheduled an appointment with an orthopedist. There was something about this doctor I just did not like. She did not appear to be concerned about his condition, and she definitely was not thorough in her examination. I told my husband he needed to find another orthopedic surgeon. So we reviewed the list again and settled on another doctor. This doctor was very caring and thorough. He examined my husband and took x-rays, including a chest x-ray (which is not routine for an orthopedic surgeon). We scheduled the knee surgery, and a few days later the doctor called and said we needed to come back to his office. Not sure why, we returned to his office a few days prior to the scheduled surgery date.

He told us that though he was an orthopedist, he had taken a chest x-ray and saw something that did not look right, so he referred the x-ray to a pulmonary specialist for review. That same day, we went to the pulmonary specialist's office. He told us he had examined the x-ray and wanted to take a few more. After carefully review-ing all x-rays, he confirmed that the spot on my husband's lung was cancer. He informed us that he wanted to do some more exten-sive tests to identify the type. Just hearing the word cancer made my body numb. I did not know what to say or think. I just silently prayed. We were told he would be fine to undergo the scheduled operation. The knee surgery went well. After the surgery, I still could not out figure out why an orthopedic surgeon had taken a chest x-ray. When I questioned him, he said he normally did not, but when my husband told him he had recently stopped smoking, he had just done it. A few weeks following the knee surgery, he was scheduled for lung surgery. The surgery was successful, and because the cancer had been caught so early, he did not need che-motherapy or radiation. I know God orchestrated this entire ordeal, from switching orthopedists to having an orthopedist take a chest x-ray to letting the orthopedist share the x-ray with his colleague who was a lung specialist. Today, many years later, he is still cancer free. Our God truly is awesome!

God also has a way of showing you that when you have faith in what He says, even when a situation might be perceived as hope-less, He can turn it around. The following situation is a prime exam-ple that shows all things that appear dismal are not, and that they can often lead to your higher good. Several years ago, my niece was evicted from her apartment. She is a religious young woman who lives and practices God's Word every day. She also exhibits strong faith; she constantly does things to help others and lead them to Jesus. However, she has gone through many hard and troublesome times. But through it all, her faith never waned. I remember one day while she was at work trying to earn enough money to support herself and her daughter, I received a telephone call from my daddy. He said she had been evicted from her apartment. She could not leave work, so I went to the apartment complex and found all her possessions sprawled on the street. I picked up what I could fit into my car. I called my husband and other family members to come and transport her things to storage. This was a difficult thing to witness; however, my niece prayed and said she and her daughter would be fine because God would make a way for them. I admired her faith. She never doubted she would rise above her present circumstance. She was not bitter; she just kept on praising and trusting in God to meet her needs and provide a way for her to get another place to stay. God blessed her with friends and family members who provided her with shelter and other necessities. Though it took several years, today she has remarried, and because of her faithfulness, God has blessed her with a wonderful husband and a beautiful home. You see, she lost an apartment, but God blessed her with a house!

The above examples should indicate to you that God does know everything you are going through and that He is always with you. He is with you through your good times, your uncertain times, and all your most difficult times. As illustrated in the poem "Footprints in the Sand," He walks with you through all of your struggles. You might sometimes wonder where God is when bad things happen to innocent people. There are so many things happening in the world today that might cause you to wonder why they are happening. Some of you might be pondering over the senseless school shootings that have occurred within recent years. Others of you might have concerns about the number of homeless people you see in your respective communities. Still others might have questions about the lack of respect, worldwide, that is being shown to people of various ethnic, religious, and cultural backgrounds. God will walk with you through your concerns or whatever situations you are going through. He and only He holds the solution to your problems and concerns. If you turn all of them completely over to Him,

He will guide you through whatever you are going through. You just need to listen for His answer and know that He will never leave you alone. Whatever questions or concerns you might have about whatever is happening around you, search for answers by participating in group discussions with other youths in the youth group at church, at youth centers, or perhaps in your classrooms to discuss solutions to these issues. You might also want to get involved in positive community activities that will address these and similar issues that have been identified in your respective communities.

I think God often allows you to go through trials and tribulations because He is trying to tell you something. While you are going through difficult times, God is working with you. He is preparing you for your good. It might be that He is toughening your skin to make you stronger. It might be that He is teaching you to lean only on Him and not to depend on your family and friends, or it might be that He is telling you to remember that He is Jehovah, the Eternal God, and the Great I Am. In your troubles, He might be telling you He is Jehovah Jireh, your provider, or that He is Jehovah Rapha, your healer; or maybe He is telling you to be still and know that He is the great Shalom and will grant you perfect peace. You know, He just might be saying to you not to worry about anything because He is El Shaddai, the God almighty of blessings, the all-sufficient God who can do anything.

There is a lesson He wants you to learn, and He will keep presenting this lesson until you learn it. What you might consider a problem could simply be God preparing you for the next blessing in your life. When you are confronted with situations you cannot handle, talk to God and seek His guidance. Once you have done what you know how to do to resolve the situation, turn it over to God and then trust Him enough to lead you to the right solution. Once you have given your situation to God, there is no need to worry. Just keep praying and have faith that He will work it out according to His will. Your trials and tribulations are a part of your growth process that will often lead to positive results.

Adverse situations that ultimately lead to victory and goodness can be seen all around you, even in nature. A beautiful example is the plight of butterflies. With their delicate wings and various vibrant colors, they glide from one flower to another with such grace, precision, and beauty. However, they did not start out this way. All growth involves a process. These butterflies start as eggs and then become caterpillars. After the caterpillars reach their full size, they become pupas. Depending upon their species, some of them spin silken cocoons around themselves or hang high on a twig or leaf in a hard, sticky liquid. They will remain in this "resting stage" until they reach adulthood. This stage can continue anywhere from a few days to more than a year depending upon their species. It looks like nothing is happening to the caterpillars, but this is a critical stage of their development. You see, while in the protective shells, the wormlike caterpillars become beautiful and graceful butterflies (*World Book Encyclopedia*, vol. 2, 619).

Like butterflies, you too will have times in your life when it seems like you are having more "ups" than "downs" and you feel as though you will never reach your goals. From this example, you should see that change is often a slow process, but in your season, you will reap your good. During your evolutionary stage, God is preparing you by ensuring that you are properly equipped to handle what He has in store for you. Do not become dismayed during this stage because it seems like nothing is happening. Know that like with butterflies, it just might take a while! In the meantime, while in your cocoon, use this time to plan and prepare yourself for the next phase. You should also know that when you have properly developed, God will move you to the next level in your life.

Throughout your life, you will experience adverse situations, but it is during these times your faith should not falter. You need to remember that adversity does produce strength and that there is a lesson to be learned in each seemingly difficult situation. Each of these important lessons will help guide you as you journey through life. Each lesson should make you stronger, more confident, and more willing to share your gifts with others. You should realize strengths you did not know you had. You should develop stronger prayer habits and be more understanding of others, more grateful, and even more caring. You should gain a greater appreciation of God's Word and willingly share it freely with others. Your life lessons should also provide you with a greater appreciation of God's Word. They will strengthen your faith and help you affirm that God is always with you, even when it appears you are at a standstill.

Related Scriptures

2 Corinthians 4:16–17 (TLB): "That is why we never give up. Though our bodies are dying, our inner strength in the Lord is growing every day. These troubles and sufferings of ours are, after all, quite small and won't last very long. Yet this short time of distress will result in God's richest blessing upon us forever and ever."

Ecclesiastes 7:14 (TLB): "Enjoy prosperity whenever you can, and when hard times strike realize that God gives one as well the other—so that everyone will realize that nothing is certain in this life."

Food for Thought/Reflections

Food for Thought:

1. Troubles don't last forever.
2. There is always a lesson to learn from your hard times.
3. Adversity produces strength.
4. You must completely turn over all your problems to God.

Reflections:

Answer each question below using examples or situations you have experienced. In your answers, talk about how you can apply the message you learned in this chapter to the examples/situations you discuss.

1. What are some adverse situations you have experienced? Describe your thoughts and feelings as you were going through these situations.
2. What lessons have you learned from the tough times you have gone through? Provide specific details.
3. What advice can you provide others to help them get through their tough times? Be specific.
4. Provide specific, detailed examples of how an adverse situation made you stronger.

FAITH FAITH FAITH FAITH FAITH FAITH

FAITH FAITH FAITH FAITH FAITH FAITH

Fruit of the Spirit

Chapter 7

But the fruit of the Spirit is love, joy, peace, patience, kindness, goodness, faithfulness, gentleness, and self-control. Against such things there is no law.

—Galatians 5:22–23 (NIV)

Now that you know life will throw a lot of things your way, you need to know God in His infinite wisdom has given you everything you need to handle anything you will face. He has blessed you with love, joy, peace, patience, kindness, goodness, faithfulness, gentleness, and self-control. These virtues, known as the fruit of the Spirit, can be applied to your daily life and help you sustain life's challenges. The moment you accept Jesus Christ into your life, you receive the Holy Spirit. As a result, the Holy Spirit changes your life to make you more like Christ. The purpose of the fruit of the Spirit is to help you exhibit the qualities of the Holy Spirit, as opposed to displaying fruits produced by the flesh. Mankind has a natural tendency to be sinful and self-centered. As humans, we are naturally drawn to things that are unlike Christ but that will satisfy the flesh, such as wrath, lust, gluttony, greed, sloth, envy, and pride, otherwise known as the Seven Deadly Sins. The fruit of the Spirit will help you be genuinely concerned about others. You can apply the fruit of the Spirit to every situation you will face throughout your life. Applying these fruits to your daily life will provide you an opportunity to show the God in you as you interact with others. Using them on a daily basis will keep you humble, appreciative, happy, and respectful of your fellow man. Let's take a look at each fruit of the Spirit.

Love

If you look in 1 Corinthians 13:4–8, you will see that love is the greatest of the fruits. According to this scripture, without love, nothing else matters. It specifically states that "love is patient, love is kind. It does not envy, it does not boast, it is not proud. It does not dishonor others, it is not self-seeking, it is not easily angered, it keeps no record of wrongs. Love does not delight in evil but rejoices with the truth. It always protects, always trusts, always hopes, always perseveres. Love never fails" (NIV). Love is very powerful. The love Jesus talked about in Matthew 22:34–40 is called agape love. This is selfless love where you love someone without expecting anything in return. It is loving others as much as Jesus loves you. In this scripture Jesus also says the two most important commandments are loving God with all you heart, soul, and mind and loving your neighbor as you love yourself. Would it not be wonderful if everyone loved unselfishly? Just think about it. If everyone exhibited agape love, the world would be much happier and more peaceful. There would be more respect for others. It would not matter where you come from, how you look, the color of your skin, or the language you speak. Can you image such a world? What does love mean to you? Think about it for a while.

While you are thinking, let me tell you what I think: God loves you so much He gave His only son, Jesus, to save mankind from sin. If God loves you this much, what is so hard about you loving one another? If He loves you this much, why do you hold grudges against others? If He loves you this much, what makes you so angry that you must settle your differences with violence? I think if you love Him, you will do as His Word says; you will love your neighbor as you love yourself. You will study and obey His Word. You will forgive others just as He forgives you. You will not kill, you will not resort to violence to settle differences, you will not steal, and you will honor and obey your parents. You will remember love is giving unselfishly and that when you truly love God, it will show in how you treat others.

According to Galatians 5:25, "If we live in the Spirit, let us also walk in the Spirit" (KJV). To me this means if God is in you and you really believe in His Word, then you will do as He instructs. Remember the game Simon Says? You only move when Simon says to do so, or you are out of the game. Well, in the game of life, you should march to the beat of God's music if you want to stay in the game. What I mean by this is that you must do what He tells you to do, you must do it when He tells you to do it, and you must do it how He tells you to do it. One major thing to remember is that all His instructions are sprinkled with love.

Joy

How wonderful it is to feel God's joy! As the Word says in Isaiah 61:10, "I will greatly rejoice in the Lord, my soul shall be joyful in my God; for he hath clothed me with the garments of salvation, he hath covered me with the robe of righteousness" (KJV). You have so many reasons to be joyous: you can rejoice in knowing that because Jesus shed His blood for you, you can live, understanding that the mere presence of God is joy. Joy is knowing the Spirit of God is upon you; it is knowing He hears and answers your prayers. God's joy is your strength.

Take a few minutes and close your eyes. Think about all the things around you that make you feel happy, that bring a smile to your face. For some of you, this could be the thought of a loved one or a special friend. For others, it could be the mountains or the ocean. Whatever brings you joy should also bring with it a secure feeling knowing none of it would be possible without God. You should never let anyone rob you of your joy.

Peace

What makes you feel at peace? Is it a special place? Is it being around certain people? Is it your state of mind? Let's talk about it. According to Webster's Dictionary, peace is "a state of tranquility or quiet; freedom from disquieting thoughts or emotions." Just take a few minutes and think about what peace means to you. What did you come up with? I am sure you have several examples.

To me, peace is a feeling I get when I turn all my troubles over to God and leave them with Him. It is knowing when I reach my limits there is someone much bigger than I am who can solve any problems, who can ease any pain, and who can work through all my "messed-up" situations. Peace is knowing that when I have done all I know to do, God will do the rest.

I remember a time on a previous job when there was a state of unrest. While I was concerned, something told me everything would be okay and not to worry. Though I was uncertain of my next step, I was at peace because I knew God had a higher calling for my life. Peace, to me, is being confident that God loves me, that He knows my needs, and that He will move in my life at the right time and in the way that is best for me. Remember in John 14:27, Jesus said, "Peace I leave with you; my peace I give you" (NIV). Bask in these words and embrace God's gift of peace. Thank you, Father, for your peace.

Patience

Do you ever notice how fast everything moves? Everyone is always on the go! Things to do, people to see! Not enough time! Can't wait! Everything has to be done quickly, fast, and in a hurry! I am sure you have been told patience is virtue. This means patience is a good thing. Can you imagine a world where people are moving at a slower pace? Where they actually take time to sit down and smell the roses and appreciate all the wonderful things God has placed on this earth for them to enjoy? It is essential to understand the importance of slowing down, how important it is to take time out of your busy schedule to notice the significant things in life. Usually these are the small things we often take for granted.

A few years ago, I lost a very dear friend, Mrs. Dorothy Ross. Prior to her transition, she sent me what was essentially a good-bye note. In this note she encouraged me to "take time to live life and to let life teach you that which is not important; there is more that is *unimportant* than you think." I encourage you to live a life of patience. Learn to wait, learn to slow down, and realize tomorrow is yet another day, and that with each new day there are new challenges, new opportunities, new hopes, and even more blessings.

Kindness

When I was a little girl, my mama always told me to treat other people the way I wanted to be treated. She told me to always be considerate of others and to respect their feelings because everyone deserves to be treated fairly. She constantly told me it did not cost anything to be kind. Can you identify with any of this? I bet your mama tells you things like this, too. I am sure you have heard this one: "you can kill a cat with kindness." This means no matter how bad someone treats you, you should be BIGGER than they are and treat them with kindness. You should show them respect; you should look beyond what they are doing or what they have done to you and see the God in them. I know it is hard to be nice to people who mistreat you, but just look at what Jesus did. He was wrongly persecuted, condemned, paraded in front of sinners, made to carry His own cross, and then was crucified. All this for no reason. Yet in spite of it all, what did He do? He asked His father in Heaven to forgive them because they did not know what they were doing. Can you imagine this? Jesus set the example. He was BIG and KIND enough to ask for forgiveness for all those who had wronged Him. So, if Jesus did all this for you, how hard could it be for you to be kind to your family members, to be kind to your friends and neighbors? Or to be kind to people you do not really know, just because they are God's children?

Goodness

Living a life of goodness is doing what you know is right. It is lifting up your brother and sister and doing everything you can to make sure you are in harmony with God's Word. Goodness is letting the Holy Spirit shine through you. When you let His goodness shine, you are living His commandments. You love your brothers and your sisters. I do not mean just your biological brothers and sisters; you also love your brothers and sisters in Christ. You love your neighbors, you obey your father and your mother, and you respect your elders. In essence, you recognize that we are all God's children and that as children of God, we all are special in our own way and each one of us is good. If you truly want to be like Christ, you will do good deeds and always recognize and respect the good in others.

Faithfulness

Faithfulness is standing on God's Word and knowing it is true. It is looking beyond what you are currently seeing, trusting in His Word, and knowing He will walk with you through the good times and the stressful times. It is knowing He will work things out for your good, according to His will. As it says in Matthew 11:6, "Blessed are those who don't doubt me" (TLB). I think this scripture demonstrates that God expects you to be faithful to His Word. Faithfulness is trusting that God will never leave you alone. When you are faithful to something or to someone, there is complete trust, devotion, dedication, and certainty. God expects these things from you in your relationship with Him.

Using God's Word as an example you should say what you mean and mean what you say. Your word should be your bond; you should want others to know that you believe what God says in His Word. You should demonstrate that you are trustworthy and that others can count on you. You should always demonstrate honesty and love and you should never doubt what God has promised.

Gentleness

Gentleness is a good virtue. It denotes kindness, calmness, and tenderness. A gentle person has strength in a lot of areas, but allows God's strength to take precedence. A gentle person follows God's lead. Some people might mistake gentleness for weakness, but it actually takes a strong person to be gentle. Several examples of gentleness can be found in the Bible. Just to name a few, Jesus was a gentle, humble person. Matthew 21:5 tells us He humbled Himself by entering Jerusalem on a donkey. Another example of gentleness is John the Baptist. As the Bible tells you in John 3:30, when John was performing baptisms to prepare the way for Jesus, he displayed gentleness when he said Jesus must become greater and greater and he (John) must become less and less. Both Jesus and John were strong people, and each of them was forgiving of others. They recognized and respected that God's words and strength were more important than theirs, so they had no problem obeying God.

Self-Control

This is also an important virtue because it allows you an opportunity to take time to think through situations and respond calmly and peacefully to them. When you exercise self-control, you allow the Holy Spirit to speak to you. In essence, exercising self-control is an effective way to guard against hasty decisions that could lead to undesirable results. In addition to providing you an opportunity to stop and think through situations, self-control can often be your best option when you are faced with circumstances that require patience and thought (as is true in most situations). Self-control can calm you down when you feel like everything is falling in around you and you cannot clearly see your way through your dilemma. Just think about it. There are many areas in your life where you can benefit from exercising self-control. Self-control serves as a defense mechanism that can guide you through unpleasant or potentially dangerous situations. It can also serve as a barrier to keep you from activities, groups, and other actions that could be detrimental to you. It can be an effective tool to use when other people are trying to persuade you to do things you know are not right. In these instances, you should demonstrate enough self-control to pull away from them and do what you know is the right thing to do.

This could be another good topic to discuss in your youth group or Sunday school class. You can also google it to find several online resources to help you gain a better understanding of how this virtue can benefit you. When you are in situations where you need to demonstrate self-control, remember that God's Word reminds you in Galatians 5:23 (NIV) that there is no law against any of the fruit of the Spirit, including gentleness and self-control.

Related Scriptures

Love

Colossians 3:14 (NIV): "And over all these virtues put on love, which binds them all together in perfect unity."

Joy

Philippians 4:4 (TLB): "Always be full of joy in the Lord; I say it again, rejoice!"

Peace

John 14:27 (TLB): "I am leaving you with a gift—peace of mind and heart! And the peace I give isn't fragile like the peace the world gives. So don't be troubled or afraid."

Patience

Ecclesiastes 7:8 (TLB): "Finishing is better than starting! Patience is better than pride!"

Kindness

Psalm 145:17 (RSV): "The Lord is just in all his ways, and kind in all his doings."

Goodness

Romans 14:17 (NIV): "For the kingdom of God is not a matter of eating or drinking, but of righteousness, peace, and joy in the Holy Spirit."

Faithfulness

Psalm 119:90–91 (TLB): "Your faithfulness extends to every generation, like the earth you created; it endures by your decree, for everything serves your plans."

Gentleness

Galatians 6:1 (NIV): "Brothers and sisters, if someone is caught in a sin, you who live by the Spirit should restore that person gently."

Self-Control

Proverbs 25:28 (TLB): "A man without self-control is as defenseless as a city with broken-down walls."

Food for Thought/Reflections

Food for Thought:

1. Love never fails. It is the greatest of the fruit of the Spirit. Everything is based upon this virtue.
2. God's joy is your strength.
3. You should always see the God in others.
4. Only God can give you peace. It is His gift to you.

Reflections:

Answer each question below using examples or situations you have experienced. In your answers, talk about how you can apply the message you learned in this chapter to the examples/situations you discuss.

1. Your main purpose in life is to love others as Jesus loves you. In what ways do you exhibit love for others? Discuss specific deeds you have done that show unconditional love.
2. What does peace mean to you? Give specific examples of times when you felt at peace. Describe your surroundings, your situation, mood, etc.
3. What does seeing the God in others mean to you?
4. Pick another fruit of the Spirit and explain what it means to you. Provide specific, detailed examples.

Your Thoughts, Your Tongue, Your Vision

Chapter 8

Fix your thoughts on what is true and good and right. Think about things that are pure and lovely, and dwell on the fine, good things in others. Think about all you can praise God for and be glad about.

—Philippians 4:8 (TLB)

once watched a person who is very dear to me drift into an ocean of negativity. As I watched my loved one sink into depression, all I heard on a daily basis was she did not have anything (even though God had blessed her with beautiful children and a loving family and several dear friends) and how everyone, except her, was doing good (in spite of the fact that she was well educated and quite intelligent). It seemed the more I tried to show her how good life was and the many ways God had blessed her, all she saw was lack, unhappiness, and defeat. I can remember telling her God is good, but she could not see His goodness because she spent all her time focusing on the things that were not what she thought they should be. I would often tell her she needed to learn to count her blessings, and if she thought life had served her lemons, then instead of sucking on sour lemons all the time, she needed to learn how to make lemonade. By this I meant she needed to stop looking at all she thought was wrong in her life and start concentrating on all the things in her life that were good.

You see, I believe that for every one thing you can find to complain about, there are at least two things you can find to rejoice about. The more I listened to her self-defeating talk, the more I realized how important it is for young people to understand the power of their thoughts and their words. You need to know that what you *think* determines what you *say*, and what you *say* determines what you *see*. This is a lesson I learned at a very young age, and I would like to take a few minutes to share my journey with you.

When I was a young girl, I was always told that I lived in a dream world. I talked a lot about what I wanted my life to be. When I was still, I could actually see myself doing the things I would daydream about and the things I often told my parents and friends I wanted to do. I had a vivid imagination and could close my eyes and see the life I wanted to live. It was like seeing a movie on the big screen and in living color! As I grew into young adulthood, and started hearing and reading about how important it was to think positive thoughts, I started to remember how my mama would always tell me "words were living things." At first, I did not understand what she meant, but the more I studied, the more I understood that it was important what I spent my time thinking about. I also understood the importance of my choice of words and how the words I chose to describe my life would shape what happened to me.

I was beginning to realize what Mama had meant. What she was telling me was I should be extremely careful about the words I used because they would determine my outcome. I realized I was not living in a dream world; I was actually seeing a preview of what my life could be, and it would only be possible if I leaned on God, had faith in His Word, believed His promises, and put my faith into action.

Maybe you will believe that whatever you spend your time dwelling on and whatever you constantly speak about will become your reality. You need to understand that your mind is a stage, and every scene should be a positive one. God's Word reminds you just how important your thoughts and words are. In Proverbs 23:7, the Word says, "For as he thinketh in his heart, so is he" (KJV). This scripture is telling you that you are what you think you are and you can do what you think you can do. You can also see the power of words in Matthew 8:16, "He cast out the spirits with his word," and in Matthew 8:26, "He arose, and rebuked the winds and the sea; and there was a great calm" (KJV).

If you are allowing life's challenges to beat you up, causing you to sink into a state of depression, just remember you can find comfort in God's Word. Search the scriptures and find one or two passages that speak life into your situation. Meditate on them. If you are a worrier and do not see your way through, you might want to meditate on Matthew 6:25–30: "Don't worry about *things*—food, drink, and clothes. For you already have life and a body. . . . If God cares so wonderfully for flowers that are here today and gone tomorrow, won't he more surely care for you?" (TLB). Maybe you are confused and do not know which direction you should go. If this is you, then you need to meditate on Psalm 37:23, which tells you, "The steps of a good man are ordered by the Lord" (KJV). If this scripture does not speak to your situation, then meditate on Psalm 23, which reminds you the Lord is your Shepard, or Psalm 27, which says the Lord is your light and your salvation. These scriptures are telling you God is always watching over you, and because He watches you, even when you think things are dark, you will always have light because you are His child and He will always be with you.

Also remember that even though your tongue is small, it is powerful. This tiny member of your body can make or break your dreams, and keep you from reaching your fullest potential. As God's Word says in James 3:5–6, "The tongue is a small thing, but what enormous damage it can do. A great forest can be set on fire by one tiny spark. And the tongue is a flame of fire. It is full of wickedness, and poisons every part of the body. And the tongue is set on fire by hell itself and can turn our whole lives into a blazing flame of destruction and disaster" (TLB). This scripture reminds you that you must learn to control what you say.

Are you beginning to understand how both your thoughts and your words can determine what you actually see? I am sure before Leonardo da Vinci painted the *Mona Lisa*, before Beethoven composed *Für Elise*, and before Michelangelo sculpted the *Statue of David*, each of these gifted people first thought about what they wanted to do and believed they were capable of doing it.

Who are some of the people in your life you admire because of the things they have achieved or the obstacles they have overcome? Is it your parents, your grandparents, a sibling, a teacher, or perhaps a neighbor? Whoever it is, sit down and talk to them. Let them know you admire their strength and stamina. Tell them why and let them tell you their personal story. In an effort to support you and inspire you to achieve your dreams, I am sure they will be happy to know they are an inspiration to you and will be proud to share their story with you. Through this interaction, you should also be able to see how the Word of God impacted their thoughts and their actions, and inspired them to continue until they achieved their goals.

With conviction and determination, all these achievers first allowed themselves to dream. With faith in their abilities, they accomplished what they thought about, and finally, with determination, they were able to see their dreams become realities. You can do the same thing if you remember to keep positive thoughts in your mind, speak to (call forth) those things you want manifested in your life, act on your faith by doing all you can to achieve your goals, and truly believe that with God, all things are possible.

Related Scriptures

Psalm 19:14 (KJV): "Let the words of my mouth, and the meditation of my heart, be acceptable in thy sight, O Lord, my strength, and my redeemer."

Proverbs 16:9 (NIV): "In their hearts humans plan their course, but the Lord establishes their steps."

Food for Thought/Reflections

Food for Thought:

1. Words are living things.
2. What you think determines what you say, and what you say determines what you see.
3. Keep your mind focused on positive thoughts.
4. Allow yourself to dream, and to dream BIG.

Reflections:

Answer each question below using examples or situations you have experienced. In your answers, talk about how you can apply the message you learned in this chapter to the examples/situations you discuss.

1. Do you believe your thoughts and your words can determine your outcomes? Provide specific, detailed examples to support your answer.
2. Explain what this statement means to you: "The tongue is a small thing, but what enormous damage it can do." Provide specific examples.
3. What advice can you provide, based on what you have learned from this chapter, to someone you know who cannot see God's goodness because he/she is focused on their perceived problems?
4. Discuss your dreams. Remember to dream BIG. What is your plan for achieving them? Be specific.

FAITH FAITH FAITH FAITH FAITH

FAITH FAITH FAITH FAITH FAITH

FAITH FAITH FAITH FAITH

FAITH FAITH FAITH FAITH

Stepping Out on Faith

Chapter 9

With men this is impossible; but with God all things are possible.

—Matthew 19:26 (KJV)

As I look back on my childhood, remembering my Sunday school classes and Bible study, I can hear my teachers saying to always keep the faith. I remember my parents constantly telling me as long as I had faith, everything would be all right. At such a young age, I was not sure I really understood what they meant. Did they mean to just be patient and wait? Did they mean what I was wondering about or worrying about would eventually work itself out? I was not at all sure. When I was about nine or ten years old, I really started to pay attention in Sunday school and had to read the Children's Bible more. I started to understand a little more about this thing called faith. As the Bible tells us in Hebrew 11:1, "Faith is the substance of things hoped for, the evidence of things unseen" (KJV). I took this to mean that you have to believe God *first* for what you want to do or for what you want to become, and if it is His will, it will happen for you. I think when God allows you to see a vision, He is really letting you know it is yours and that all you need to do to make it a reality is have enough faith to go for it.

As a child, one story that helped me to understand faith is found in Matthew 14:23–31. In this story, Jesus had fed the multitudes and told His disciples to get into the boat and go to the other side of the lake while He helped the people to get home. After He finished, He went to the hills to pray. When night fell, Jesus knew His disciples were in trouble because the winds had gotten high and the waters were rough. As the ship was tossed by the stormy, heavy waves, Jesus walked to His disciples on the rough water. This frightened His disciples because they thought He was a ghost. Jesus told them not to be afraid. It was then Peter said, "Lord, if it is you, tell me to come to you on the water." Jesus simply said, "Come," and instantly, Peter got out of the boat and started to walk to Jesus. Remember, Peter was in a boat, so when he started to walk, he was actually walking on water, too! I don't think Peter was aware of what he was doing; he just started to walk—faith. Can you imagine what the other disciples might have been thinking? They were probably thinking things like, *Peter, are you crazy? You can't do that! What makes you think you can walk on water? Get back in the boat before you drown. If that really is Jesus, He will come to you.* As long as Peter focused on Jesus and acted on faith, he was fine. He sank only when he lost focus and started to doubt what Jesus told him to do. This act of faith proves no matter what you are going through, as long as you hold steadfast to God's Word and keep your focus on Jesus, you will make it through even what you think is a most difficult time.

Who had more faith than Job? Remember when God allowed Satan to test his faith? Job lost everything he had, including his children. No matter what Satan threw at him, Job never lost faith in God. Even his wife told him he should curse his God and die. As a result of his faithfulness, God blessed him with more than he had before.

And what about Sarah and Abraham? It had to take a lot of faith to believe that at her age, she could conceive a child. It was their strong faith in God's promise that He would do whatever He said He would do. Sarah was past the childbearing age, and Abraham was too old to father a child, but because of their faith, a nation of countless people was born.

Another one of my favorite acts of faith is when the people of Israel obeyed God's command and walked around the walls of Jericho for seven days. The walls tumbled down, allowing them to enter into the Promised Land.

Of all these biblical examples of faith, my favorite one is the story of Abraham and his son Isaac. Genesis 22:1–19 tells us that God told Abraham to sacrifice Isaac, his beloved son, as a burnt offering. Abraham obeyed God and took Isaac to Mount Moriah, where he prepared the altar and then bound Isaac and placed him on top of the wood. Just as Abraham took out his knife and was ready to plunge it into Isaac, the Angel of God called out to him and told him to put his knife down and not to hurt his son. As he was putting the knife down, he noticed a ram that was caught by its horns in a bush. Instead of sacrificing his son, he used the ram as a sacrifice. This was Abraham's proof that God will always provide. This moment proved Abraham truly loved God and that God was first in his life because he would not withhold his beloved son from God. This is truly faith in action. This act of faith proved Abraham's obedience and love for God. His actions made his faith complete. Abraham's act of faith demonstrated that when you have faith and obey God, He always provides for you. Because Abraham, the father of faith, trusted God enough to offer his son as a sacrifice, God blessed him, his many descendants, and all the nations on the earth.

As I grew older, probably around twelve or thirteen years old, I started to ask a few more questions and actually began to study a little. I learned there was more to faith than just believing in God's Word. I learned it has another essential dimension. This important aspect of faith is called "works." This means you must put your faith into action and do what needs to be done. At this point, I realized this was exactly what Abraham had done. Wow! It was really starting to sink in. I was beginning to realize that having faith is no good if you do not actually do something to effect a change. Both faith and works go together like a hand and a glove. They work in tandem with each other, meaning you can have faith, but at the same time, you must act on whatever it is God tells you to do. Faith is standing up firmly for something you believe in. It is embracing something you truly want to accomplish and knowing what the Bible says in James 2:17: "It isn't enough just to have faith. You must also do good to prove that you have it. Faith that doesn't show itself by good works is no faith at all—it is dead and useless" (TLB).

To reinforce the biblical examples and help you better understand the concept of faith in action, and how it relates to your world today, let's look at things currently happening around you. Two major yet distinct marches occurred in 2017 and 2018 that visually demonstrated what faith in action looks like. Both these protests involved bringing national and worldwide attention to situations many people in the United States and throughout the world believed were unfair. They decided to take action against them.

The first were the women's marches that brought attention to issues that adversely impacted women's rights, including respect in the workplace, unequal pay, unfair promotional opportunities, etc. These successful marches were originally planned as national marches on Washington, DC, but they received worldwide attention for advocating women's rights. Approximately 2.5 million women peacefully participated in the women's march.

Though the women's marches were successful, the 2018 March for Our Lives protest is the one you can really identify with. It was planned, organized, and successfully orchestrated nationwide by young people like you! WOW! You might even have been one of the organizers! Though incidents involving gun violence have previously occurred on college campuses, universities, movie theatres, and night clubs throughout the nation, the surviving teens of a mass school shooting at Marjory Stoneman Douglas High School in Parkland, Florida, successfully put their faith into action. As a result, these teens organized a peaceful protest that brought national attention to the senseless act of gun violence. The protest focused on the growing number of children who are being killed in elementary, middle, and high schools throughout the nation. Though this protest started as a national focus, it gained worldwide support.

Prior to the March for Our Lives protest, these students also successfully demonstrated faith in action by organizing a nationwide Student School Walkout Day. To show solidarity for the cause, a massive number of students in elementary, middle, and high schools throughout the United States (at the designated time) walked out of their respective schools in protest.

Your generation is stepping up in massive numbers to address issues that will require a continued demonstration of faith in action.

As you move forward and together in solidarity to bring focus and action to your consolidated plans, remember to keep God first and He will direct your path.

I now understand this thing called faith. I know you cannot have faith and doubt at the same time. To me, faith means believing God's Word; it is standing on His promises. It is being bold enough to stand tall, even when things are at their worst or when you are at your weakest. It means believing God will provide. You see, when you have faith, nothing stands in your way. You are focused on what you are trying to do. You do not think about failing, because when you have faith, failure is not an option. I now understand faith is more than believing you can accomplish something; it is being so strongly convinced you can achieve your goal(s) that you actually step up and do it!

If there are things God has spoken into your spirit, you should not worry about what others will think or say. Some people might think you are crazy, but only you know what God has spoken to you. Dare to grab hold of your dreams. I encourage you to rise above your self-imposed limitations and doubts, and dare to become all God says you can become. Step out on faith and put your faith in action to move toward your good.

Related Scriptures

2 Corinthians 5:7 (KJV): "For we walk by faith, not by sight."

James 2:17 (TLB): "So you see, it isn't enough just to have faith. You must also do good to prove that you have it. Faith that doesn't show itself by good works is no faith at all."

Food for Thought/Reflections

Food for Thought:

1. Faith and doubt cannot exist at the same time.
2. When you have faith, failure is not an option.
3. There is always a "ram in the thicket." In other words, God always provides.
4. Faith is no good without action.

Reflections:

Answer each question below using examples or situations you have experienced. In your answers, talk about how you can apply the message you learned in this chapter to the examples/situations you discuss.

1. Explain what faith means to you. Provide examples of when you have acted upon your faith. What were your results?
2. Have you ever been in a situation where you could not see your way out, and then suddenly options you had never considered were made available? Explain your "ram in the thicket." What was the outcome?
3. What are some of the issues you see around you right now that are good examples to show how faith followed by action leads to good results?
4. What does it mean to walk by faith, not by sight? Give examples where you have actually done this.

Epilogue

Go Forth!
A Challenge to Teens

Be dressed ready for
service and keep your
lamps burning.

—Luke 12:35 (NIV)

Thank you for reading *#BOUNDLESS: Realizing the God in You.* I pray it has been an inspiration to you. I hope you agree that you are a child of God and are connected to the Holy Spirit through Jesus Christ. You should now affirm that you are capable of climbing any mountain, be it real or self-imposed, and of overcoming any obstacles in life. Through God's love and His power, you can accomplish great things. When faced with life's challenges, just still your mind and body and allow God to work through you. You see, once you put "self" aside, it is true that you can do all things through Christ who strengthens you. When you invite the Holy Spirit to come into your life, in essence you are inviting God to take full control. You are letting Him be captain of your ship. You are telling Him you accept His guidance and that you will abide by His Word. You are telling Him you are yielding to His power. It is when you truly let go and let God that you will see tremendous changes and growth in your life. It is imperative that you remember He is omnipotent, omnipresent, and omniscient. This means He is a powerful God; He is everywhere and He knows everything. You should also remember He is just a prayer away and you need only to call Him up and tell Him what is on your heart. He is still in the blessing business, and He is waiting to hear from you.

I challenge you to stand on His Word and promises and to believe they will not return void. If God said it, believe it, and take Him at His Word. Trust in Him and realize He wants you to step into your purpose. Realize He has predetermined a specific role for you, a role that cannot be filled by anyone else. Realize He purposely created you to be who you are and that you are created in His image, and therefore you are good, perfect, and whole.

Allow God to work through you. Every day of your life, you can be an example of His goodness. Stand up for what you believe and let God fight your battles.

As a teen today, you are the seed of the generations to come. Learn God's Word and be willing to share it with others. Being a child of God means you are your brother's keeper, and therefore, you have the responsibility of leading others to Christ. Help them understand it is okay to praise Him and it is okay to acknowledge Him. Be a strong voice for God's kingdom. Show others how to use His Word to solve problems as opposed to violence. Help your peers understand that they should open their minds and hearts to find better solutions, and that with God, they can bring harmony into violent situations. Remember what Romans 14:19 says: "Let us then pursue what makes for peace and for mutual upbuilding" (RSV). This scripture simply means that because of your connection to God, you have a flexible mind and can choose good over bad, and you also have the discernment not to follow your peers who are not walking in God's path.

When you are faced with situations in life you cannot understand, just remember Proverbs 3:5–6: "Trust in the Lord with all your heart and lean not on your own understanding; in all your ways submit to him, and he will make your paths straight" (NIV). Do not be ashamed to talk to your friends about God's goodness and how He has brought you through. Be the shining light that will lead your wayward friends to God. Tell your friends it is good to go to church. His Word says where two or three are gathered in His name, He will be in their midst. Tell them it is also okay to become involved in positive community activities. Let them also know God is love and He will always love them, unconditionally.

Let them see His good works in you. This can serve as an inspiration to them. Let your friends know that according to 2 Corinthians 5:17, "If any man be in Christ, he is a new creature: old things are passed away; behold, all things are become new" (KJV). This means it does not matter where they came from or what they did in the past. All that matters now is they have found God and have been born again because they believe Jesus Christ died for their sins and was resurrected, and that God's spirit lives in them. Is this not a beautiful message to pass on to your friends and acquaintances? God has blessed you so you can be a blessing to someone else.

I challenge you to go forth and continue to glorify your Heavenly Father by reaching out to others and helping to lead them to Christ. You can start by getting involved in student and community organizations. If none are available in your school or community, take the initiative and organize them yourself. You can participate in Sunday school or get involved in the youth ministry at your church. You can also use electronic media to start a focus group. There are countless other ways you can reach out to others. Whichever approach you choose, I pray you will "always be doing those good, kind things that show you are a child of God, for this will bring much praise and glory to the Lord" (Philippians 1:11, TLB).

To God be the glory! Amen.

Related Scriptures

Deuteronomy 5:33 (NIV): "Walk in obedience to all that the Lord your God has commanded you, so that you may live and prosper and prolong your days in the land that you will possess."

John 14:6 (KJV): "I am the way, the truth, and the life: no man cometh unto the Father, but by me."

Food for Thought/Reflections

Food for Thought:

1. You can do all things through Christ who strengthens you.
2. You should be a strong voice for God's kingdom.
3. It is your responsibility to help lead others to Christ.
4. You need to develop a plan of action to become a strong voice for God's kingdom.

Reflections:

Answer each question below using examples or situations you have experienced. In your answers, talk about how you can apply the message you learned in this chapter to the examples/situations you discuss.

1. How can you use what you have learned from this book in your daily life?
2. What strategies do you have for being a strong voice for God's kingdom?
3. What can you share with others that will let them know God is not concerned about their past, that once they accept Jesus, they become anew?
4. How can you use God's Word to help put a stop to the gun violence that is so prevalent in our society?

Instructor's Guide

The purpose of this guide is to provide interactive games and other methods of delivery that will enhance students' learning experiences. This guide is also developed as a suggested starting point for Sunday school classes, youth retreats, and youth group meetings. In an effort to ensure students understand the message discussed in each chapter, instructors should remember that students have different learning styles and are, therefore, encouraged to incorporate their own creative ideas into the learning process. Learning is fun! Engage your students and encourage them to share their ideas and experiences.

Chapter 1:
Understanding Who You Are

We are all God's children, no matter how we differ from one another. One way to teach this chapter is to have students pair up with someone in the group who they think is like them. Have them take a few minutes to discuss why they think they are alike, then have them pair up with someone they think is different from them. Allow them to discuss their differences. Then ask them to see one another through God's eyes and discuss what it means to be a child of God.

Key items to discuss include:

- Are our visible differences important?
- What Christlike qualities do we all share?
- Are we more alike than we are different? Explain.

Another way to teach this chapter is to allow the students to use music or poetry. They can create positive rap songs or use the spoken word to demonstrate their understanding of the information presented in this chapter.

Chapter 2:
Understanding God's
Purpose for Your Life

For this chapter, ask students to write down what they think their purposes are. Then ask them to discuss what they wrote. Include the following in your response:

- How do you know this is really your purpose?
- When did you realize this was your purpose?
- What steps will you take to make your purpose a reality?

Ask for volunteers to share their thoughts.

Chapter 3:
The Importance of Prayer

This chapter can be approached in a variety of ways:

- Since prayer is so private, this chapter can be approached as a period of reflection, where students can take a few minutes to think about how prayer has made a difference in their lives.
- Another strategy can be to have students write how they view prayer and why they think it is important to them. They can write or engage in a group discussion concerning situations in their lives or in the lives of close friends and/or relatives where prayer made a difference.
- Still another approach can be asking for a few volunteers to sit on a panel (a mock TV talk show) to talk about various components, such as why it is important to pray, how God taught us to pray, how people in the Bible effectively used prayer, and how unexplainable things can happen as a result of prayer.

Chapter 4:
Hearing from God

The purpose of this chapter is to help students understand the importance of being quiet and still. They need to learn how to relax and how to get in tune with their inner strengths. Any activity that affords them a chance to sit and focus will allow them to experience their oneness with God.

To relax the body and mind, the instructor can do relaxation exercises. These can include basic beginning yoga poses and also meditation. To set the mood, make sure you dim the lights, light scented candles, or use pastel-colored lightbulbs and play calming music. Suggested music includes but is not limited to:

- Classical
- String instrumentals
- Smooth jazz
- Nature sounds

Since the sound of water is soothing, you can also use serenity fountains.

Once your students are relaxed and focused, it is then time to engage them. You can pair them up and have them alternate asking one another to describe an instance where they were faced with a difficult decision or challenge they thought they could not handle but realized once they relaxed and focused on God, and not on their situation, they were able to reach a viable solution. Ask them to share with the group. This exchange should generate discussions.

Another suggestion can be a group activity where teams are formed. Each team should not exceed five members. Each team will be asked to present a situation in the Bible that was resolved when the person stilled himself/herself and listened for God's solution. Have them discuss how they can relate to these situations.

Chapter 5:
Dealing with Spiritual Warfare

Christian movies can be great resources. You can select movies that discuss topics such as:

- How to deal with temptation
- Settling differences without violence
- Recognizing and dealing with the struggle between good and evil
- Understanding how to make good decisions, including how to decide between right and wrong
- Lessons Jesus taught about love, obedience, faith, and righteousness.

Another activity could be to divide the students into small teams and present different real-life scenarios and ask them to develop solutions based upon biblical principles. Let the students be creative in their methods of delivery. The only requirement is that every team member must participate.

Chapter 6:
Learning through Adversity

To assist your students in understanding that throughout their lives, they will encounter problems, and that life is a series of ups and downs, they can play the following games I have developed to reinforce the lessons taught in the book.

Game 1: Anything Is Possible with God

Objective:

The purpose of this activity is to demonstrate that God sometimes allows you to go through difficult times, but if you believe His Word and do as it says, then you will survive. You can choose to play specific songs in the background that relate to faith or overcoming difficulties or whatever you think is appropriate.

Procedure:

This game is based upon a series of obstacles. Groups work together as a team to discuss solutions (based upon biblical principles). Each team should include no more than five members. This should allow each member an opportunity to participate in the team's discussion. Participation should be stressed at the onset. The instructor should move throughout the room to ensure each team member participates and also to observe the discussion. Each team should identify a recorder who will write the team's responses. Paper and a marker will be provided to each team.

The instructor can develop obstacles that deal with school issues, family issues, dating, gun violence, or any other adverse situations that impact today's youths. The obstacles are placed in a box labeled

"Life's Ups and Downs." The instructor will ask one student to pull from the box. The instructor will then read the obstacle that was chosen. Each team is then challenged to discuss the obstacle (i.e. why they think it is an obstacle, what situation(s) in the Bible they can relate this obstacle to, and how this or a similar obstacle was resolved in the Bible). In addition, they should develop at least three lessons they can learn from the hardship(s) encountered. As the instructor, you can allow as much time as you think is needed for this activity. The instructor can also allow students to present their results in creative ways (i.e. dance, skits, song, poetry, etc.)

Game 2: The Adversity Challenge

Objective:

This is another game that can be used as a teaching tool to illustrate how adverse situations were handled in the Bible.

Procedure:

Each team will consist of five players. Each team will also identify a team captain. The questions will be based on events in the Bible. The instructor will compose and ask each question, and the team that hits the buzzer first will have a chance to answer. There will be five rounds played, each with ten questions. Each question is worth ten points, except in the final round, where the questions will be worth twenty points each. The team with the most points at the end of the final round will win the game.

Chapter 7: Fruit of the Spirit

I developed the following game, entitled fruit of the Spirit, as a fun way to understand what the fruit of the Spirit is and how it can be applied to life.

Objective:

- To understand that God has blessed everyone with the fruit of the Spirit.
- To demonstrate how each fruit can be applied to everyday situations.

Procedure:

- Divide the class into small teams (include no more than four groups with no more than five people in each team).
- Each team will select one person to pick a piece of plastic fruit from a bag or basket.
- Each piece of fruit will be inscribed with one of the eight fruits in Galatians 5:22–23. To ensure students understand each fruit, the person pulling from the bag or basket will not be able to see the inscriptions. If allowed to see the inscriptions, students might pick the one they know best, thus limiting their understanding of the others.
- Each team will have twenty minutes to develop a three-minute jingle, skit, song, dance, etc. to show how the fruits they have chosen can be applied to everyday situations. Be creative, but make sure you base your presentations on Christian values.

Props:

- A green vine (plastic or silk) will be mounted on the wall with push pins or masking tape.
- As each team starts its presentation, one of the members will clamp his/her piece of fruit on the vine before continuing with their presentation. (This signifies John 15:5: "I am the vine and you are the branches.")
- At the end of the presentations, each team member can select a piece of fresh fruit from a fruit basket.

Chapter 8:
Your Thoughts,
Your Tongue, Your Vision

The purpose of this chapter is to help students understand that their thoughts and words do shape their worlds. Suggested exercises are listed below:

1. One exercise to help reinforce the power of their thoughts and their tongues is to ask students to review the autobiography of someone they admire. Let them use the internet or other resources to research artists, musicians, and some people who have made history and see if they can identify how the person's thoughts, words, and/or visions shaped their lives.

2. As a contrast, have the students talk about people they know who they think have promise, but who are negative, complain all the time, etc. What are some examples of how this person's thoughts impacted his/her life? As a result of what you have learned, what can you tell this person about the relationship between his/her thoughts, tongue, and vision? How did the person's life turn out?

3. Allow students to discuss how their own thoughts and words have impacted their lives. Include both positive and negative impacts.

Chapter 9:
Stepping Out on Faith

Each of us can remember a time when we were not quite sure what to do, how to do it, when to do it, or even if we should do it. The following suggestions should provide students with opportunities to share experiences that demonstrate times when they stepped out on faith.

1. To reinforce the lesson taught in this chapter, the instructor is encouraged to discuss a time when he/she was not sure what to do but trusted God and stepped out on faith. The purpose is to help students understand that during each of their lives, they will need to exhibit faith in God's Word. Even though they do not know what to expect, they must learn to step out on faith and to lean on God.

2. Once the instructor has shared personal experiences, divide the class into small teams. Each team will include four members. Each team member will present one of his or her teammate's experiences to the entire group. Youth will have approximately fifteen minutes to share their experiences. This exercise should show examples of the various situations that require faith in God to move to the next level or to overcome tribulations.

Epilogue:
Go Forth! A Challenge to Teens

So where do you go from here?

This challenge can lead to a discussion on what each student either sees as his/her personal role in furthering God's kingdom or what they as a generation can do to ensure God's Word is shared. In addition, students can also list how they will tell others about the power of God's Word and of His goodness.

Another step to determine where they (as an individual or as a generation) can go from here is to divide into small groups to review and discuss their answers to the reflection questions at the end of each chapter. As a group, discuss some of the answers. This could provide a starting point to executing a plan of action that can make a difference.

Bibliography

Munroe, Myles. *Understanding the Purpose and Power of Prayer*. New Kensington, PA: Whitaker House (2002).

Nelson, Thomas. *What Does the Bible Say about . . . The Ultimate A to Z Resource to Contemporary Topics One Would Not Expect to Find in the Bible*. Nashville, TN: Thomas Nelson, Inc., 2001.

The Life-Study Fellowship. *With God All Things Are Possible!: A Handbook of Life*. New York: Bantam Books, 1990.

World Book Encyclopedia. 22 vols. Westlake, OH: Scott & Fetzer, 1985.

About the Author

Cassie F. Palmer has a passion and gift for helping young people realize their potential. She has been applauded for her ability to encourage and motivate youths. Her educational background, church involvement, and professional experiences have provided her with the foundation for this book.